Kerry Parnell

Kerry Parnell is a journalist and has worked in magazines and newspapers for ten years. She has edited teenage magazines in Britain and Australia and now works in the women's glossy magazine market as a writer and editor. This is her second book for teenagers. She lives in Surrey.

Street Smart

A Teenager's Guide to Being Sussed and Safe

Kerry Parnell

First published in Great Britain in 2002
by Piccadilly Press Ltd.,
5 Castle Road, London NW1 8PR

A catalogue record for this book is available
from the British Library

ISBN: 1 85340 756 9 (trade paperback)

1 3 5 7 9 10 8 6 4 2

Printed and bound in Great Britain by Bookmarque Ltd.
Design by Fielding Design
Cover design by Judith Robertson

Set in 10.5pt Palatino, Helvetica, Rotis Sans and Tempus

Contents

Introduction

'Be aware, not beware'

This book is for anyone, male or female, who'd like to be safe.

Every day you hear of someone in the news, who's had their bag snatched, their pocket picked, or far worse. It's difficult to imagine what you'd feel like, or do, if something like that ever happened to you.

Don't panic. I'm not saying that anyone who *doesn't* read this is going to get mown down by a lunatic in the next five minutes: most people make it through their whole teenage and adult lives safely. But unless you've been living in the *Big Brother* house your whole life, you'll know that there are plenty of hazards out there – most of them in the form of other people.

It makes sense to know about all the problems you may have to face, so if you did ever find yourself in a dodgy situation, you would know what to do. And that's what this book is for.

Being a young adult today can mean facing a bewildering array of choices – good and bad – and often you feel like no one else quite understands what it's like out there. So in this book I have tried to cover every eventuality you can possibly think of: from online safety, to safety on the streets. The book covers partying problems, such as drink and drugs, through to how to get home safely. But it also talks about issues in the home and at school, because it's not simply strangers that can bring problems into our lives. And finally, it covers crime and how it can affect you: what to do, what to say, and how to get help.

This book aims to empower you, to give you all the tools you need to be confident in everyday life. You see, confidence is our biggest weapon – it's free, available to everyone, portable and flexible. It works whenever and wherever you need it: be it on a date, fending off a fight, or coping with crime.

Use this book however you want to – dip in and out of chapters that seem relevant to you right now, or those you'll need for the future. Or you could steam through the whole lot and become super-sorted in one go – it's up to you! But however you use it, whether to prepare yourself, or to help your friends, before or after an event, it should help you to become aware of the realities of all sides of life.

And remember – just because you're aware of problems in life, it doesn't automatically mean they'll happen to you. In fact, the more you know and the more aware you are, then the less likely it is they ever will.

The message is *be aware*, rather than *beware*.

Socialising

Chapter 1

Peer Pressure

In Hollywood films peer pressure is always so simple – new girl joins school, tries to fit in, but doesn't get picked for the cheerleader squad, so instead makes friends with the weird girls who wear Goth outfits and appear to be into witchcraft. Cheerleaders hate witchy girls, witchy girls hate cheerleaders. Cue big kerfuffle usually to do with boys, when witchy girls suddenly have to rescue cheerleaders. All are saved, they become friends and dance off together like Britney Spears.

But real life, as we know, is nothing like this, and peer pressure is far less straightforward. It isn't even always bad – it's a good feeling when your friends agree with the way you see things, such as liking the same music, clothes and celebs. You feel accepted, confident, and 'normal'. You might want to expose your mates to the same experiences. Or you could enjoy a bit of healthy competition with your mates – for example, 15-year-old Marie's best friend was really good at English, so Marie made it her mission to be even better, and ended up getting A's in the process. Steven was really good at cricket, so he got all his friends into it too – years later, he gave up, but one of his mates now plays professionally. If his friend hadn't had that kind of good peer pressure, he probably never would've played.

But, of course, not all peer pressure is so positive, and that's what this chapter is for – to help you figure out what to do if you think you're suffering from negative peer pressure: how to avoid it, what to say, and even how to stop pressuring someone else.

Stuart's smoking dilemma

The group of friends I hang around with at school smoke, and I don't. They don't really mind, but lately they've started smoking weed. I don't want to look lame by not puffing so I've done it a few times. But now one of my mates has been caught at school with cannabis, and has been excluded, and my mum's on my back about it, saying I can't see them any more. It's really hard to know what to do.

Stuart, 14

Stuart's story is a good example of peer pressure. He doesn't care if his mates smoke, and they don't care if he doesn't. He's confident enough in himself to do what he wants. But now he's faced with two problems:

1) Stuart's mates have moved on to cannabis, which means they're out of it, while he just feels left out.
2) It's gone pear-shaped for him, as not only has the school excluded his mate and tarnished Stuart with the same offence, but his mum's found out, and thinks his friends are a proverbial 'bad influence'.

What would you tell Stuart to do?

a) Carry on seeing his mates, and smoke if he wants. He can always sweet-talk his mum.
b) Tell his mates he doesn't want to see them any more and make friends with 'Brian-no-buddies'.

c) Try to have a chat with his mum, explain that he understands where she's coming from, but these are his friends, and he promises he'll be careful and not get into anything dodgy.

You could pick any of these answers because the right answer is the choice you really want to make about how to live your life. The point is, it should be YOUR choice, and not something you're forced into doing just to fit in.

Whatever pressure you face from your mates, remember that there are MANY ways to live your life. You have the right to live however you want.

It's best to avoid situations where you're not comfortable. Never try something because someone's telling you, 'Go on, chicken.' Your body and mind have warning systems for a reason. So if you're scared, it's usually an indication that you are facing a dangerous situation.

While it may seem harder to speak up for yourself and disagree with everyone else's opinion, in the long-run, it may be the best thing you'll ever do.

What is negative peer pressure?

Negative peer pressure happens when your friends, peers, class or school influence you in a negative way. For example:

1) You feel like you're not accepted unless you have the latest phone, computer, game or gadget.
2) You feel left out unless you have the right clothes, shoes or hairstyle.
3) You feel square if you don't drink, smoke, do

drugs, or have sex as much as your peers.

4) You think you'll look soft if you don't shoplift, vandalise, joyride, bunk off or get detention like your mates are doing.

But what if I want to do some of these things?

That's entirely up to you – no one can stop you. Just make your own decisions, know they are for the right reasons and be aware of the consequences. If you think the best thing you could ever do in your life is to nick a car, get arrested and land a criminal record, then it's not likely this book would stop you. OK, that's an extreme example, but whatever choices you make, just be sure that you know *why* you are doing them. If the answer is, 'Because my mates are doing it,' then think some more. You only have one life: live it for yourself, on your own terms.

Help! I'm a 'peer pressurer'!

Q: *Who are the people that pressure others?*
A: We are.

Can you honestly say you've never put pressure on your mates – good or bad? Really? We all have a lot of influence on each other, and sometimes you don't even know that you can affect others' lives so much. When 16-year-old Liz's best friend told her she'd lost her virginity, Liz asked, 'Really? What made you decide so suddenly?' Her friend said, 'Because you have, so I thought I would get on with it.'

And Andrew, a hyper-brainy friend of Tim and James, all 14, once answered a whole page of questions wrong in a maths exam, just so he could stay in the same set as them, as they'd been annoyed that Andrew would have to move classes. Both of these cases were due to peer pressure, and the friends didn't even know they were doing it.

Tip: If you think you might be influencing a friend to do something that you don't feel is right for them, then stop. Think about your motives – are you doing it to make yourself feel better? Do you want to feel reassured that you are all 'in it together'? Having the same outlook is good: shaping someone into something they're not is bad. Be big, be brave, be different! Be yourself.

Coping with peer pressure: Do's and Don'ts

Do say no in a pleasant and confident way. Explain you're not really into whatever they're doing, saying or offering. Actually you prefer something else, but thanks anyway. Show them you can see their point of view and are tolerant of them, so they should be tolerant of you.

Don't start lecturing people against whatever it is they are doing.

Do be careful how much you influence your friends.

Don't make it a competition between your view and others' views.

Do have confidence in yourself. You can look, act, feel or think differently from your peers and still be friends with them. It is allowed.

Don't do something simply to 'fit in'. Make sure you're 100% happy to do whatever it is, and that you've thought it through.

Do talk about it. If you feel uncomfortable with the direction your friends are going, then be honest. Express your opinion fairly and try to reach a compromise.

Don't keep things to yourself. If you feel seriously worried about something, then seek help, from your parents, teachers, or even a helpline (see Resources). Bottling up problems only makes them worse.

Do give your parents the benefit of the doubt. They may be a bit out of touch with the scene that faces you, but actually, they are not that off the mark. They may not know what K is (see Chapter 3), and they may think Status Quo are still in the charts, but they want you to get through your teen years in one piece, and . . . (drumroll please) . . . they have been through similar situations themselves.

Don't think that your friends (or enemies) hold all the secrets to the universe, and you don't. They are just as freaked out as you by all the choices facing them – just as insecure, confused and worried. Yes, they too sit in their rooms listening to deep song lyrics, they too feel the pressure to try new things, or take new risks. (They might just never *tell* you).

Be aware: Peer Pressure

In summary, here are the main points to take away from this chapter:

1) Not all peer pressure is bad.
2) You could be a peer pressurer yourself and not realise it.
3) Bad peer pressure is anything that influences you in a negative way.
4) You are responsible for your own actions and decisions.

You have the power to decide the course you'll take.
5) If you are seriously troubled by peer pressure, then seek help. Talk to someone you trust, or contact a helpline (see Resources).

Chapter 2

Alcohol

Quiz: Are you a 'thinker-drinker' or a 'boozer-loser'?

How much do you really know about drinking? Take the following test to find out if you've got a lot of bottle or are out for the count.

Simply tick True or False after the following statements:

1) Men can drink more than women. T ☐ F ☐

2) A 'unit' of alcohol equals a half-pint of beer. T ☐ F ☐

3) If a man drank four pints a day, he'd be within his 'recommended daily limit.' T ☐ F ☐

4) If a woman drank four glasses of wine a day, she'd be within her 'recommended daily limit.' T ☐ F ☐

5) Alcohol dehydrates you. T ☐ F ☐

6) Alcoholic drinks with bubbles make you drunk quicker than those without. T ☐ F ☐

7) It's good to mix drinks – it makes you get drunk quicker. T ☐ F ☐

8) The higher the percentage of alchohol in your drink, the harder you are. T ☐ F ☐

9) If you're out with friends, you have to keep up with their pace. T ☐ F ☐

10) The more you drink, the more your body gets used to it, so you can safely drink even more next time. T ☐ F ☐

How did you score?

Check your answers below and score two points for every correct answer.

1) True, **2)** True, **3)** False, **4)** False, **5)** True, **6)** True, **7)** False, **8)** False, **9)** False, **10)** False.

0–6 Boozer-loser – Oh dear, you wouldn't know a booze-truth if it slapped you in the face, and you're so fact-addled, you're nearly unconscious. But fear not, resuscitation is at hand. Simply read this chapter closely, and you should revive and survive.

8–14 Half-pint – You're nearly there. You know most of the facts, and can spot an old wives' tale across a crowded bar. But some of the details are a bit blurry, so gen up on the facts and fantasies below, and you'll be top of the glass in no time.

16–20 Thinker-drinker – Well done! You really know your stuff when it comes to booze. You may be able to tell the difference between a Moscow Mule and a Vodka Redbull, but it's always worth refreshing yourself with a swift chapter and a packet of facts.

The truth about booze

Booze-truth 1: Most people in this country enjoy a drink – the amount of pubs and bars around show you how much of a national pastime it is!

Booze-truth 2: Drinking can make a night out really fun, relaxing everyone and putting them in a good mood. It's perfectly safe and good fun, as long as you control it.

Booze-truth 3: When you do lose control and get really drunk, you can be:

a) the life and soul of the party
b) over-emotional and really upset
c) aggressive
d) Mr Lover Man or Woman
e) mouthy
f) sick
g) passed out
h) all of the above and more, in any order . . .

This chapter is your ABC of alcohol, so you can get the facts, make them work for you and never lose to the booze . . .

What is alcohol?

Alcohol is produced by fermenting fruits, vegetables or grains. It is found in drinks like beer, wine, alcopops and spirits. Alcoholic drinks range in strength, and the alcohol content is measured as a percentage. The higher the percentage, the stronger the effect.

The common types of alcohol are:

- beer, lager, bitter, cider
- white wine, sparkling wine, champagne
- red wine, port, sherry
- spirits – vodka, gin, whisky, etc.
- liqueurs – Baileys, Cointreau, After Shock, etc.
- cocktails – These are a mix of spirits and sometimes liqueurs, as well as fruit juices or cordials (e.g. Piña Colada, Cosmopolitan).
- alcopops – These are spirits mixed with something soft, like lemonade (e.g. Bacardi Breezer).

How is alcohol processed in your body?

When you drink, about one-third of the alcohol is absorbed through the stomach wall. If you have eaten a lot before drinking, then this slows down the process. The rest of the alcohol is absorbed through the small intestines into the blood stream, where it reaches all parts of the body – the brain, nerve cells, etc. Your body burns up the alcohol as energy, and this can take as many hours as the amount of drinks you've had.

Diet note: While the body uses booze-calories, it stores all your food calories for the future. So that's why, if you drink a lot, you put on weight.

How much can I drink?: The facts

Fact: Men can drink more than women.
Before all the female readers start complaining, there is a good reason for this. Women's bodies have more fat tissue and less water than men's, so the alcohol is more concentrated in theirs.

Fact: The less you weigh, the more concentrated the alcohol you've drunk will be in your body.
Therefore, a tall, thin person may get more drunk than a short, fat person.

Fact: If you space out your drinks, you'll get less drunk.
For example, if you drink three glasses of wine in an hour you'll be more drunk than if you drink the same amount over three hours.

Fact: Your mood can change the effect of alcohol.
If you feel very emotional, for example, you might feel drunk very quickly.

Fact: Food in your stomach slows down the alcohol's effects.
This makes you less likely to feel sick. Drinking on an empty stomach is not a shortcut to a good night out.

What is a unit of alcohol?
One unit equals a half-pint of beer or a small glass of wine or one measure of spirit.

What is the legal drinking age?
Selling alcohol to anyone under 18 is illegal. But if you are 16 or older you can have a drink with a meal in a restaurant.

Binge-drinking
Q: *If I don't drink all week and then have 10 beers on a Friday night out, is this OK?*
A: No. The above figures are an average over the week. Drinking it all or more in one go is called binge-drinking, and is not healthy or safe.

What are the recommended daily limits?
Men: No more than three units a day (one and a half pints of beer or three glasses of wine) or you run the risk of serious health problems.
Women: No more than two units a day (a pint of beer or two glasses of wine).

Drinking and driving
It sounds complicated, but the legal limit for driving in the UK is 80mg of alcohol per 100ml of blood. It takes

different people a different amount of drink to reach this level, but the safest advice is not to drink any alcohol if you are driving. Failing that, one half-pint of lager, or one small glass of wine is the maximum. NEVER take the risk of driving if you are over the limit, and DO NOT get into a car with a driver who's over the limit – no matter how much alcohol they say they can handle.

According to the Institute of Alcohol Studies, young people's tolerance for alcohol is lower than adults'. At the *legal* alcohol limit, an adult is twice as likely to have a road accident, but a young driver is FIVE times more likely.

Real-life story: 'I missed my own party'

It was my birthday party and I was really excited. It was fancy dress and I had on this mini-dress and my hair in a beehive. It was such a laugh. We made punch in a bucket in the kitchen, and added whatever anyone brought round. I had about ten big glasses of it. I was dancing away, when suddenly I felt dizzy, and blacked out.

Apparently, I'd gone into an alcohol-coma, and my friends had to call my parents and the doctor, and the party was cancelled. I got taken to hospital with alcohol poisoning, and had my stomach pumped. The doctors said I could have died. It was the worst experience of my life.

Shauna, 17

Medical fact: Severe drunkenness is far more harmful medically to teenagers than adults, because teenagers need to drink less alcohol to go into a coma, develop hypoglycaemia (low levels of blood sugar), hypothermia and breathing difficulties.

What happens when you get drunk?

1) The good side: You might think everything's hilarious. For example, telling jokes, having a sing-a-long with your mates, and dancing the night away. You could feel less shy, more confident, and up for a good time.

2) Motor-mouth: Your mouth might get a life of its own, and you might start blabbing secrets, or picking a fight for no reason. Or you might feel so great that you tell everyone, and I mean *everyone*, you love them – the barman/woman, your mate's boyfriend/girlfriend, the smelly old man in the corner . . . See where this is going?

3) Pulling power: Yes, straight to point three, where before you know it, you've pulled. And congrats, it's Mr/Mrs Personality Bypass of the Year. And all your mates have clocked you.

4) Down and out: It could make you depressed. Alcohol is a depressant, so if you're feeling down, it might make you feel worse.

5) Sick of it: It can make you ill. You might start feeling sick, you might actually start being sick – even right there in the middle of a party. Sometimes your body just violently expels the alcohol if you can't cope with it, meaning that you ruin your outfit, you look gross, and your mates have to drag you home.

6) Hangover hell: And then there's the morning after – pounding headache, nausea, vomiting, all of which can last well into the next day.

7) Deadly: Most frighteningly, though, it can actually kill you. Getting very drunk can lead to loss of consciousness. Once passed out, you risk choking to death on your own vomit. And drinking too much can lead to alcohol poisoning, which can also kill.

Scary statistics

1) Young people are the heaviest drinkers in our population. According to the charity Alcohol Concern, 50% of males and 41% of females aged 16 to 24 drink above **the safe limit** (see page 20).

2) And guess what? Young people here are also the heaviest drinkers in Europe. According to the 1999 European School Survey Project on Alcohol, British teenagers topped the charts for binge-drinking, drunkenness and alcohol problems. Great! Not.

3) Drink-driving is the cause of 1 in 7 deaths on the roads in the UK.

4) Around half of all pedestrians over 16 killed in road accidents have been drinking.

5) 40% of violent crimes are linked to alcohol.

6) Alcohol accounts for at least 7% of drownings.

7) Nearly half of all household fires are linked to people who've been drinking.

8) About 1,000 teenagers under the age of 15 go to hospital with serious alcohol poisoning each year.

9) People who have sex after drinking are much less likely to use condoms.

10) According to Alcohol Concern, 40% of 13- to 14-year-olds said they lost their virginity because they were drunk or stoned. For more information, see Chapter 5.

Long-term alcohol problems

Long-term mega-boozing can be seriously bad for your health. If you drink way more than the recommended limits every day for a long time, chances are good that you'll put on loads of weight, get high blood pressure, increase your chance of having a heart attack, stroke, liver damage, cancer or emotional problems.

Alcoholics in the family

An *alcoholic* is someone who is addicted to alcohol. If someone in your family is an alcoholic, this can be really hard for you to cope with, and can have far-reaching effects on your life. The first thing to remember is that it's not your fault, and second, you can get them help. For more information on addiction, see Chapter 3.

Alcohol: Do's and Don'ts

Do drink slowly. Pace yourself, and keep a check on how much you drink.

Don't have a drinking race with anyone. Everyone has a different tolerance level, and you don't need to keep pace with others to look cool – just skip a round.

Do make sure you've eaten enough before you go out. A kebab at midnight won't 'soak up the booze', it's too late by then.

Don't do anything you wouldn't do if you were sober, i.e. do you really fancy them?

Do drink a soft drink or water in between each alcoholic drink. It dilutes the alcohol and helps prevent dehydration, stopping you from getting too drunk, or ill.

Don't ever mix drink with drugs. Alcohol slows down your body's nervous system and if you mix it with other drugs (see Chapter 3) or medication, you run the risk of shutting down your body altogether.

Do stop drinking alcohol immediately if you feel sick or dizzy. Start drinking plenty of water.

Don't drink a really strong drink like strong beer or cider, a cocktail, punch or neat spirit just to look 'hard'.

Do remember that alcopops may taste nice, but are just as strong as other drinks.

Don't guzzle alcopops like lemonade because you're thirsty.

Do drink plenty of water before you go to bed, to avoid dehydration and sickness.

Be aware: Alcohol

In summary, here are the main points to take away from this chapter:

1) It's unhealthy to drink more than three units a day for men, and two units for women.

2) You're more likely to be involved in a car accident after just a few drinks.

3) Teenagers are less tolerant of alcohol than older people.

4) Never do anything when you're drunk that you wouldn't do when sober.

5) Never mix alcohol with drugs.

Chapter 3

Drugs and Addiction

Whatever you think of them, whatever you do with them, it's likely that everyone will come across some sort of drugs today. But how much do you really know about drugs? Unlike alcohol, the word 'drugs' covers a huge group of substances, that all do different things to your body. Some are deadly, some are much less dangerous. There are no lectures here. The purpose of this chapter is to arm you with the facts – it's up to you what you do with them.

What are drugs?

Drugs work in different ways, depending on their ingredients, your mood, how much you take, and your exact mental make-up. But in general, there are four broad 'types' of drugs, which are:

1) Stimulants: These can increase your brain activity, making you more alert and energetic. They are also known as 'uppers', e.g. speed, cocaine.

2) Depressants: These are the opposite of stimulants, and slow down brain activity, making you more relaxed. They are also known as 'downers', e.g. alcohol, tranquillisers, solvents.

3) Hallucinogens: These are drugs that distort the mind, making you hallucinate (see or hear things you wouldn't normally do), e.g. LSD, magic mushrooms, cannabis, ketamine.

4) Analgesics: These have a painkilling effect, making you feel 'knocked out', e.g. heroin, morphine, opium.

Note: Some drugs can be a mixture of these types, such as ecstasy, which is a stimulant and a hallucinogen.

Drugs and the law

Categories: In the UK, drugs are divided into three classes – Class A, B and C, with A being the highest, and having the strongest penalties. Sometimes, drugs can move categories – the law is always changing.

Possession: If you are caught with a small amount of drugs on you that you claim are for personal use, this is termed 'possession'.

Intent to supply: If you are caught with an amount of drugs that the police and courts say is more than for one person, this will categorise you as intending to supply other people, so the penalties are much higher.

Factfile: Your A–Z of drugs

Amphetamines

Common Names: Speed, dexy's midnight runners, meth, base, ice, glass, uppers, whiz billy, sulph.

Type: Speed is a grey, white or dirty-white powder which can be snorted, dissolved in liquid for injection or drinking, or found in a pill form. It's the most impure illegal drug available in the UK.

Effects: Amphetamines are a stimulant. They quicken the heartbeat and breathing rate so the user becomes more outgoing, lively and talkative. The user often has tension in their jaws – so they look like they are chewing. Amphetamines were used as slimming pills in the 1960s because they reduce appetite, but are extremely dangerous, as the body does not get enough nourishment.

Dangers: Addiction, anxiety attacks, depressed 'comedown' for up to three days, memory loss and strain on heart. They can also cause mental illness. If you have the slightest risk of schizophrenia, amphetamines can push you over the edge. Mixing with ecstasy can put too much strain on the heart and cause your body to overheat. Overdosing can cause death.

Legal Classification: Class B, but Class A if injected.

Amyl nitrate, or poppers

Common Names: Liquid gold, high-tech, rave, rush, ram, thrust, locker room, snappers, hardware, rock hard, kix, TNT.

Type: Poppers is a term for a group of chemicals, that comes as a liquid in a small tube, which you inhale. Amyl nitrate is just one of these chemicals – Butyl nitrate is used more often in the UK and is usually found at clubs or raves.

Effects: They were originally invented as heart medication, so they cause a sudden rush of blood to the heart followed by light-headedness. The effects last for about five minutes, and you often get a headache afterwards.

Dangers: Repeated use can cause headaches, sickness, dizziness, or make you pass out. The chemicals can burn the skin if you touch them and can cause death if you swallow them.

Legal Classification: They are classed as a medicine, so possession is not illegal, but it's an offence to supply them.

Cannabis

Names: Marijuana, draw, blow, weed, puff, shit, hash, black, ganja, spliff, brown, dope, fatty, gear, green, harry monk, henry, 'erb, pot, solids, skunk, bud.

Type: Cannabis is a natural substance from the marijuana plant (often called hemp). Resin is a solid dark lump, while grass is dried leaves, stalks and seeds. It is smoked with tobacco or on its own, in a pipe or a bong and can also be eaten. There are different strengths of cannabis – some varieties are very strong.

Effects: Users feel relaxed, talkative and giggly. Eating it can make the effects more intense, but harder to control. Users could feel sleepy or very hungry.

Dangers: Short-term memory loss, increased chance of accidents as you have a lack of co-ordination, can make you paranoid and anxious. If mixed with alcohol, can cause nausea and vomiting. High doses can cause mild hallucinations and smoking may increase the risk of lung cancer. It also can be addictive.

Legal Classification: Class B.

Cocaine and crack

Common Names: Coke, charlie, crack, rock, snow, barley, cheng, clam chowder, gack, toot, sherbert, blow.

Type: Cocaine is a white powder made from the leaves of the coca plant. It has powerful stimulant properties similar to those of amphetamines. People usually 'snort' cocaine through a small tube, up into the nose. Soluble cocaine is sometimes injected or mixed with heroin (a dangerous mixture called a 'Speedball'). Crack is a smokeable form of cocaine.

Effects: Feelings of well-being and euphoria for about half an hour, followed by a 'come-down' which can make you feel anxious, depressed or unable to sleep. A crack high is more intense, but shorter. It's also highly addictive, which makes you want to take more and more.

Dangers: Deep and quick addiction to cocaine and crack, sneezing, nosebleeds, damage or even disintegration of the nasal membrane, lung damage, fatal overdose possibilities.

Legal Classification: Class A.

Note: With any drugs that you inject, remember that sharing needles puts you at high risk of catching HIV and Hepatitis or gangrene.

Ecstasy

Common Names: E, pills, doves, X, disco biscuits, bruce lee's, jack dee, jack and jills, knobbly knees, echoes, hug drug, burgers, fantasy.

Type: Ecstasy is made up of a mixture of chemicals, including a drug called MDMA, and is classed as a hallucinogenic amphetamine. Usually white in colour, it comes in tablets of different shapes and sizes. Different ecstasy tablets contain different amounts of MDMA, while some have none at all.

Effects: Feel a rush of nervousness and heart races, when 'come up'. High energy and enhanced feeling of empathy with other people. Sound, colour and emotions more intense. Can dance for hours. Effects can last 3-6 hours.

Dangers: Intense sweating, tightening of jaw – can overheat and dehydrate. Paranoia, confusion. Can feel depressed and tired after use, for days. Can cause brain damage or death. Impossible to know what each tablet contains – some can be mixed or 'cut' with dangerous chemicals.

Legal Classification: Class A.

GBH/GHB

Common Names: Liquid E, liquid X.

Type: Gamma-hydroxybutyrate (GBH/GHB) is a clear liquid that comes in bottles or capsules, or can be drunk. It was originally invented as a medicine for people having surgery.

Effects: It is a sedative, so can bring on a state of euphoria and make you feel more sociable. Effects can last for a day.

Dangers: It is very difficult to take the right dose as strengths vary, so it is easy to overdose and die. Mixing with alcohol or other drugs can be fatal. It can cause sickness, convulsions, coma and seizures.

Legal Classification: It is legal to possess it, but illegal to supply it.

Heroin

Common Names: Smack, skag, horse, junk, brown.

Type: Heroin is a painkilling drug made from morphine, which comes from the opium poppy. Heroin is a brownish-white powder, which users snort, smoke, or inject.

Effects: Small doses can give you a deep sense of warmth and well-being, along with nausea or vomiting, especially soon after injecting. Larger doses can lead to drowsiness, and excessive doses can result in an overdose, coma or death.

Dangers: Extremely addictive, habit can quickly get out of control, and tolerance develops so you need more heroin each time. Sharing needles can put you at risk of HIV, hepatitis and gangrene. It is very difficult to give up. Overdose can result in coma or death.

Legal Classification: Class A.

Ketamine

Common Names: Special K, K.

Type: Ketamine is an anaesthetic with painkilling and hallucinogenic properties. It comes in tablet, liquid or powder form.

Effects: It numbs the body, and makes you feel removed from reality. Can have 'out of body' experiences, hallucinations and temporary paralysis.

Dangers: Increased risk of injury, as you have no feeling. Breathing problems, unconsciousness, heart failure, choking. Very dangerous if mixed with other drugs or alcohol. Can make you vomit, or choke on vomit if you lose consciousness. Can cause death.

Legal Classification: It is a prescription-only medicine, so not classed like other drugs, but if supplying it may carry Class C penalties.

LSD

Common Names: Acid, sugar, trips, tabs, sid, bart simpsons, blotter, micro dots, liquid.

Type: Lysergic Acid Diethylamide (LSD) is an hallucinogenic drug that comes in tiny squares of paper, often with a picture on one side. Microdots and dots come in the form of very small tablets.

Effects: It has a powerful effect on your mind – making you see objects move, distort or hallucinate. The 'trip', can be different each time and may last for 8 to 12 hours. You can get flashbacks of past trips for a long time afterwards – sometimes months or even years.

Dangers: Once the trip starts, there's no way of stopping it. Bad trips are common and can be terrifying – you may see horrific images and think they are real for hours. Dizziness, disorientation, fear, paranoia and panic. Accidents may happen while hallucinating. Also, if you have any psychological problems such as depression, anxiety or schizophrenia, LSD can make these problems worse.

Legal Classification: Class A.

Magic mushrooms

Common Names: Mushies, happies, sillies, shrooms, purple passion, caps.

Type: Magic mushrooms are types of mushrooms that produce hallucinations when you eat them.

Effects: Similar to LSD. Users have a short 'trip' of about four hours where they can feel spaced-out, euphoric and hallucinate.

Dangers: Stomach ache, sickness, 'bad trips' are common

– and once on a trip you can not stop it. Trips can cause serious mental problems and you could risk death if you eat a poisonous mushroom by mistake (and many deadly mushrooms look like magic mushrooms).

Legal Classification: When dried, cooked, boiled or prepared in any way to be used as a drug, they are Class A.

PCP

Common Names: Angel dust, ozone, wack, rocket fuel, peace pill, elephant tranquilliser, dust.

Type: Phencyclidine (PCP) is a white crystal powder which people inject, sniff, smoke, or swallow.

Effects: It is a hallucinogenic drug which can make you feel dreamy. It's well known for causing very bad trips.

Dangers: It is often mixed with other drugs. It has extremely strong side-effects – bad trips are common, and people can feel aggressive, paranoid and cause harm to themselves or others. For example, people jump to their deaths, or drown, while on PCP. It can also lead to severe mental problems – even after small doses. Large doses can cause kidney failure, breathing problems, convulsions and death.

Legal Classification: Class A.

Solvents

Common Names: Glue sniffing, huffing, solvent abuse.

Type: Solvents can be found in household items such as lighter gas refills, fuel canisters, aerosols (i.e. hairspray, deodorants, air fresheners), tins or tubes of glue, paints, thinners and correcting fluids. They are sniffed or breathed into the lungs.

Effects: Feels like being drunk for a short time. It slows down heartbeat and makes you feel 'fuzzy-headed', dreamy and sometimes dizzy and giggly. May vomit or hallucinate. Effects last about half an hour and headaches are common afterwards.

Dangers: Sniffing solvents can kill you – even your first time, as can spraying solvents down your throat. They can cause damage to your nasal membrane, and you can suffocate if using a plastic bag to breathe in. You are more prone to accidents when high, and long-term use can cause damage to your brain, liver and kidneys. Sniffing to the point of unconsciousness means you can choke on your own vomit and die.

Legal Classification: It is illegal to supply solvents to persons under the age of 18 if someone knows, or suspects, that the product is intended for abuse.

Discussion board: Drugs

The following are a few thoughts and opinions on drugs. What do you think?

I smoke dope with my friends sometimes. I don't see what the problem is with it. I don't think it's any different to drinking, and I think it should be made legal.

Renny, 16

My brother started doing a lot of acid a few years ago. Then, all of sudden, he started acting really weird – talking about people on TV telling him to do things. His girlfriend left him, he lost his job, and now he's been certified schizophrenic. He went into a mental home for a while, but he's still no better. The doctor said that it depends on the person – you could take just one trip, or whatever and it could do this to your brain. I don't do drugs now – seeing what happened to my brother makes me too scared. I don't think he'll ever go back to how he was before.

John, 15

When we go clubbing, we always take E. Everyone I know does it. I don't believe all the scare stories about it.

Ellis, 18

I have been taking speed for a year, but recently I had my first bad experience. My heart started pounding so badly that I thought I was having a heart attack, and my head felt weird. I sat in the loo for half an hour, being sick. I was OK, but I've gone off the pills now.

Helene, 16

Last week my friend drove his car after he'd done a couple of bongs. He crashed through someone's front garden, and injured his girlfriend who was in the car with him. He doesn't drive any more after he's been smoking.

Simon, 18

It's your choice

1) Get the facts: Have the information, then make the choice. Read as much as you can about drugs – here and elsewhere – see Resources for more information sources.

2) Know more than your mates: Just because your friend says something's safe, it doesn't make them an expert! To be really clued-up, you have to know the facts for yourself.

3) Have an opinion: Whatever you decide to do, to use drugs or not, make the decision for the right reason. Going with the flow, and doing something for no other reason than the crowd is doing it, isn't being true to you.
4) Respect: It's all down to respect. If you respect others' decisions, they'll respect yours. You can still fit in, by standing by your beliefs.

Addiction in the family

My sister is a heroin addict. She has been one for 10 years, and always comes round to beg money off our mum. If we give her money she spends it on drugs, if we don't she starts going mental and screaming at us, and sometimes she steals things from the house. Mum has tried to get her into rehab six times but she always leaves. It's all we ever think about.

Rhiannon, 14

Dad has a drink problem. He's lovely when he's sober, but after he's been drinking he's violent to me and my sister, and mum. He makes my life a misery – all I want is a normal dad so I can bring friends home and not be ashamed.

Scott, 16

Unfortunately some of us have to cope with members of our family, or friends, who develop drink or drug addictions. The reality is that for every addict, there are friends and families who suffer. And when it's you suffering, it can feel scary and lonely.

How do I know if they're an addict?

The answer is simple. If someone's drinking or drug use

(prescription drugs or illegal) is causing you a problem, then it is too much. Drinking too much or using too many drugs is like a disease. Once someone starts they can't stop. It makes them act strangely, get into fights and do things they never would do if they were sober. Ask yourself the following questions:

1) Do you worry about how much they're drinking?
2) Do you try to cover up their drinking or drug taking?
3) Have you ever felt angry about their drinking or drug taking?
4) Do they have a drink or take drugs first thing in the morning?

If the answer to any of these questions is yes, then they may have a problem.

What can I do?

1) Accept that when someone is drunk or high, this is not necessarily their true personality, just like if you've seen your mates act stupid when they have been drunk.

2) Know that people who are addicted want their next hit of drink or drugs above anything else. They can't think about anything else but this – it controls their lives.

3) Remember YOU ARE NOT TO BLAME. No matter what you have done, you can't make someone have an addiction. You can't make them stop on your own. But you have to look after your own life – if they are affecting you mentally or physically, like if they are violent towards you, then you have to get help as fast as possible.

4) Talk about it: Once you have come to terms with the

problem, you will find that there are many people who suffer in the same way. It's good to talk about it, with friends, family, a doctor, counsellor or teacher. You can also get help from telephone helplines such as the National Drugs Helpline, Drinkline or Alateen – a special organisation for young people affected by someone else's drinking (see Resources).

5) Have fun. This may sound silly, but it's important that you don't surround yourself in misery all the time. Go out with your friends, play sport or join a club, and do something on your own terms to make yourself feel better.

6) Get them help. Encourage your parent or sibling or friend to get help – to go to their doctor, or join groups such as Alcoholics or Narcotics Anonymous. Many of these groups have family therapy units, where you can all talk through what it's like living with this problem. You may think that sounds scary – but they really can help.

Telephone helplines

If you would like more information on drugs and addiction, or need help for yourself or a friend, there are many organisations that can help, such as The National Drugs Helpline, Release and Alcoholics and Narcotics Anonymous. See Resources for contact details.

Be aware: Drugs and Addiction

In summary, here are the main points to take away from this chapter:

1. Drugs affect you in a variety of ways – they are all different.

2. Different people may react differently to the same drug.

3. Know the facts – your mate's advice is not always the best.

4. Know the law – you can't plead ignorance if you get caught.

5. If a friend or family member has a problem, remember that it's not your fault. You can't help them on your own, but you can get the help you need.

Chapter 4

Dating

Real-life story: 'It's not that scary!'

I really fancied this guy called Adam for months, and eventually he asked me out. I said yes, and we arranged to meet in town on a Saturday night. I was so nervous. Before this, I hadn't really been out on a proper date – my last boyfriend had just been part of our group of friends, so we didn't really go anywhere without everyone else. I didn't know what to expect, or what to wear, so in the end I just turned up in jeans and tried to act normal. We went to the cinema and then got a burger afterwards, and he walked me home. I was nervous for no reason – I had a really good time.

Sienna, 14

Too much pressure!

There was this girl at college that I really liked, but I just didn't know if she fancied me or not. Anyway, one day I asked her if she wanted to go out with me, and she said yes. So we went out to a club, and had a real laugh. I walked her home, we kissed, and then things went a bit further, and she said she wanted to have sex with me. I thought this was a bit quick, and didn't know if I really wanted to sleep with her yet – I wanted to get to know her a bit more. I said this to her and she said I wasn't a real man, and laughed at me. We went out once more, but it wasn't the same, so it ended. I still don't know if I did something wrong – I just didn't expect all that pressure on my first date.

Damon, 17

The dating game

The Good: Going on a date with someone can be really exciting – your heart starts thumping, girls spend five hours perfecting the 'natural look' make-up, boys spend four hours getting that perfect gel effect, and you feel like you're walking in 3 metres high inflatable trainers, you've got that much bounce in your step.

The Bad: Then there's dating when you a) haven't done it much, b) don't know what you're meant to do, and c) are worried you'll look like a div.

The Ugly: And then there are the few times it all goes pear-shaped, and you end up on a date from hell! They don't turn up, you don't get on, they expect more than you do, or you change your mind in the middle of it and need to make a sharp exit.

The seven steps to successful dating

Worry not, all you need for disaster-free dates are the following seven steps:

Step One: Going out, getting home

Sounds odd, but the first thing you need to do is arrange how you'll get home (see Chapter 6 for more details). It's essential you know how and what time you'll get back. Ask your parents (cringeworthy, but easy) to meet you at a certain place and time, book a taxi, or arrange to come home with a friend. Whatever you decide, you should always make sure you're safe. If the date goes well, maybe you'll walk home together, or catch the bus – but if it doesn't, always carry enough money for an emergency cab ride home. Never walk home alone.

Step Two: A right looker

It's up to you to wear whatever you feel comfy in. It's obviously best to try to match the outfit to the occasion. (That sequin party dress or designer suit might seem a bit out of place go-karting, don't you think?) Just wear whatever you think best represents you – your personality and taste. It's never a competition, and it's not about how much you spend either – people who carry off their clothes with a personal sense of style always look more attractive, whatever brands they are wearing. Plus, if you feel comfortable in your clothes, you'll be more relaxed on the date.

That said, it's probably best not to wear your sexiest or most outlandish outfit on a first date – unless you know the other person REALLY well. No one wants to look like the weird one from *Blind Date*, after all.

Step Three: Blind date back-up

Blind dates can be very exciting – you've never met the person, you don't know what the date may bring. If you decide to go on one, it's best to arrange to go with someone else – if you were set up by a friend, invite them along and make it a group thing. If you met the person on your own – like over the internet – then the same applies. See Chapter 9 for more information on internet dating. It's not wise ever to meet anyone on a blind date on your own, without having someone go with you to at least check that they are OK. Arrange to meet somewhere you are familiar with, tell your friends and family where you are and what you will be doing. Stay in a public place at all times, and don't go off with them in their car, or to their house, for example, until you are certain you know them well enough. Again, make arrangements ahead of time for getting home.

Step Four: The X-factor
This is the mysterious chemical reaction that means two people actually 'click'. Because however sexy, nice, funny or fit the other person is, sometimes you just don't click, no matter what you do. It's the spooky world of 'lurve', and there's nothing we can do about it.

There's nothing worse than getting to the end of the night and thinking, 'It's just not happening,' while they're gazing into your eyes, planning the wedding reception and naming your babies. You'll know if you fancy them, as you just feel it. If you do, then wayhey, off you go. If you don't, you need to be honest. (Secret: Loads and loads of people end up having a snog because they're too embarrassed to say they don't want to, and feel sorry for the other person. But who'd want to be on the receiving end of a mercy snog?) If they want to kiss you and you don't want to kiss them, then say, 'I'm sorry, I'd rather be friends,' or, 'No, I don't want a snog,' or something like that. Yes, it's embarrassing, but it's much better than lying. If they still try, then push them away, and if they still try, get out of the situation as quickly as possible.

Step Five: No obligation
If a boy buys a girl dinner, does that mean she owes him a snog, or more? What do you think the answer is? It's amazing, but some people still think that if a boy takes a

girl out and buys her anything, then she owes him at least a kiss, if not more. Obviously this is ridiculous, no one buys someone's body with a meal – or anything else.

Likewise for the rules of dating. Basically, if you are on a date, this doesn't mean you're obliged to do anything. You might want to kiss or you might not. You might want to go further, or you might not. You don't have to do anything you don't want to, and it doesn't matter how many times you've been out with someone, or what 'signals' they say you have been giving them. You could date someone for years and never sleep with them if you wanted! Never feel obliged to do anything you're not ready to do, even if you think you want to and then change your mind.

Tip: Say no, clearly and with conviction. If you find yourself in a compromising situation with anyone who starts pressuring you, then get yourself away from them as quickly as possible. See Chapter 5 for more information on sex.

Step Six: Keep control
Finally, a good date is one where you know what you are doing. Don't drink so much or get so out of it that you are not in control of yourself. No matter how wild you feel, if you lose all control you won't know what's happening to you – good or bad. Have a great time, but remember the great time. If you do feel like you are losing control, the best thing to do is leave. Tell your date you want to go home, call a taxi, your friends or family. Make sure you get home safely, though – see Chapter 6 for more details.

Step Seven: Your get-out clause

A cunning but effective strategy is to hatch a 'get-out' plan before you go out. This way, if you think the date is not going well, you can put your plan into operation and make a sharp exit. Try these:

a) The urgent call: Arrange for a friend to call you on your mobile at a certain time and if you want to leave you can say, 'Oh no, my mate's boyfriend/girlfriend has dumped her/him, I'll have to go and see her/him.'

b) The secret text: You text someone to call you, or turn up and 'bump into you', so rescuing you from the date.

c) The back-up event: Find out where your other friends are going to be, and then if the date's deadly, you can suggest going to see them, where you can join the crowd, and let someone else talk to them.

They may sound cruel, but they work!

Be aware: Dating

In summary, here are the main points to take away from this chapter:

1) It's important to know how you're getting home, before you go out.

2) Always meet blind dates somewhere public, and tell someone else where you are going.

3) Expectations are made to be broken – if you don't 'click', you can't force it.

4) Keep control – too much drink or drugs can make you go from cool to fool in seconds.

5) Wherever you are, whatever you've done – if you get cold feet on a date, then walk them right out of there.

Chapter 5

Sex

Quiz: Are you a 'sexpert'?

Are you a love learner, or a sex master? Simply tick True or False after the following statements:

1) The Pill protects against STIs.   T ☑ F ☐
2) There are condoms made for women.   T ☑ F ☐
3) Sex makes you more mature.   T ☑ F ☐
4) You can catch AIDS from loo seats.   T ☑ F ☐
5) Women can get pregnant during their period.   T ☐ F ☐
6) Men's testicles get firm when they are sexually excited.   T ☐ F ☐
7) The clitoris is outside the vagina.   T ☐ F ☐
8) Women can't get pregnant the first time they have sex.   T ☐ F ☐
9) If a man is turned on and doesn't have sex, his balls will turn blue.   T ☐ F ☐
10) Women and men always orgasm during sex.   T ☐ F ☐

How did you score?

How much do you really know about sex? Check your answers below and score two points for every correct answer:

1) False, 2) True, 3) False, 4) False, 5) True, 6) True, 7) True, 8) False, 9) False, 10) False.

0-8: Sex-lies – Someone needs to pay a bit more attention in sex class, if they're going to pass the love exam. You wouldn't sit your driving test without ever taking a lesson, so it's worth separating the facts from the fiction when it comes to sex, before you make any mistakes.

10-14: Sexercise – You know the basics – and you're no love fool. But some of the details are a bit misty, and you're not always able to tell your sex myths from your sex facts. Before you do anything physical, you need to get literal, and fill in the missing info in your love dictionary.

16-20: Sex-wise – Well done, you're top of the love class. You've made it your business to find out as much as you can about sex, and filter out the froth from the facts. Remember, though, you can never know too much – knowledge truly is power, and the only way to get more knowledge, is to keep learning.

Let's talk about sex

Sometimes it seems like all anyone talks about is sex – on the telly, in the newspapers, even on *Top of the Pops*. We're either doing too much of it too young, doing it with the wrong people, or doing it with a celeb and then telling the world about it. So what's the big fuss?

There's no getting around the fact that sex is natural. It's normal. And almost everyone will do it, at some point in their lives. If people didn't have sex, then we wouldn't be here, would we?

Although it sounds stupid to say this – don't forget that sex does equal making babies. Obvious, yes, but many people forget this fact. Britain has the highest teenage pregnancy rate in Western Europe – figures show that although British teenagers don't necessarily have more sex than say, the Dutch (who we think of as very liberal), they use less contraception, and therefore have more pregnancies. (According to the Family Planning Association, one survey showed that half of under-16s having sex used NO contraception at all.)

Add to this the scary fact that teenage Sexually Transmitted Infection (STI) rates are BOOMING in Britain, and you can see the results when you don't use protection. So in all, it's much less embarrassing to be prepared, than caught out.

Are you ready?

Sex can be a wonderful experience when you're in a loving relationship, both parties are fully aware of what they are doing, and you're physically and mentally prepared. But take away any of these factors – and the balance is upset. For example, if your partner isn't looking for a relationship and you are, or if you get carried away on the spur of the moment and don't use contraception, problems can arise. Ask yourself the following questions:

1) Are you in a serious relationship?
2) Do you trust each other?
3) Will you feel 100% happy about your actions tomorrow?
4) Do you love each other?
5) Have you talked about sex?
6) Have you discussed contraception?
7) Do you have any contraception?

8) Do you understand how STIs are transmitted?
9) Are you over 16 years old?
10) Do you think you are emotionally ready to cope with sex in your relationship?

If you answered no to any of these questions, you may need to slow down and ask yourself if you are truly ready to have sex. Sex changes relationships – it doesn't make them better or worse, and it doesn't solve any problems, but it takes your relationship to a more complicated level. It leaves you and your partner vulnerable to getting hurt, if things go wrong.

Sex and the law

There's one important factor for anyone under 16 years old thinking about having sex. It's illegal. You probably think this a daft law – like how's anyone ever going to know? It's not as if you have to buy a 'sex-please' license from a shop, or anything, but the law is there to protect you, as most people under 16 are still working out what's happening to their lives, bodies and relationships. Therefore, having sex too soon could be damaging to your body and your brain as you may not be physically or emotionally ready. According to the law, if females have sex under under the age of 16, they can't be prosecuted, but males can be prosecuted, even if she consented to sex.

Note: If you are under 16 and are determined to have sex, then see your doctor or clinic to arrange contraception. They don't have to tell your parents. Never take a risk with your health.

Contraception

Contraception is the prevention of pregnancy. Before you even think about having sex, it's vital that you understand the types of contraception available, discuss these options with your partner, and then go to your doctor or clinic to arrange contraception.

Remember: You need to protect against STIs *and* pregnancy, not one or the other. If you are on the Pill, for example, it's best also to use a condom, to protect against STIs.

The following is a short guide to the types of contraception available at clinics such as the Family Planning Association or Brook clinics.

Condom

The condom is a thin latex 'sleeve' that covers a male's erect penis and catches sperm inside it during sex. Condoms are free from Family Planning Clinics or can be bought in any chemist or pub toilet. A condom protects against pregnancy *and* STIs.

Female condom: This is a similar 'sleeve' that fits into the vagina and catches the sperm during sex. It's more expensive than male condoms, but also protects against STIs and pregnancy. Both condoms are 85-98% effective.

The Pill

There are two types of contraceptive pill – a combined pill and a progesterone-only pill. Your doctor or clinic will advise which type is best for you. The combined pill is a mixture of the hormones oestrogen and progesterone.

It stops females from producing an egg each month. It's almost 100% effective at contraception. The progesterone-only pill thickens cervical mucus, making it hard for the sperm to swim up the fallopian tubes. It also makes the womb inhospitable for a fertilised egg. Both pills are very effective, but neither protect against STIs, so a condom should also be used.

Diaphragm or cap
This is a soft rubber disk that fits at the top of the vagina and covers the cervix. A diaphragm is fitted by a doctor and when used with spermicide, prevents sperm entering the cervix. It protects against some, but not all, STIs and is 85–96% effective at contraception.

Contraceptive injection
Women can get injections like Depo-Provera from their doctor. It consists of the hormone progesterone, which then disrupts the production of eggs and the menstrual cycle. The injection lasts about three months and is 99% effective at contraception. It doesn't protect against STIs.

Contraceptive implant
This implant consists of six hormone capsules that are surgically inserted into your arm, which stop the production of eggs, and hinder sperm movement. It works for five years and is 99% effective at contraception. It doesn't protect against STIs.

IUS
The Intrauterine System (IUS) is a small plastic device that

contains progesterone, which is fitted into your womb by a doctor and slowly releases the hormone. The IUS thickens the mucus in the cervix, helping to stop sperm reaching an egg, and making the womb inhospitable to an egg. It works for at least three years and is almost 100% effective at contraception. It doesn't protect against STIs.

IUD

The Intrauterine Device (IUD), also known as a coil, is a small plastic and copper device that is fitted into the uterus by a doctor and works by helping to stop sperm meeting an egg, or by preventing an egg from settling in the womb. It works for about five years and is about 98% effective. It doesn't protect against STIs.

Morning After Pill (emergency contraception)

For information about emergency contraception see page 57.

Sexually transmitted infections (STIs)

Unfortunately, sex isn't all moonlight and candles, romance and rose petals. It also has a rather unpleasant side. Sexually transmitted infections are common amongst teenagers. You're probably thinking, 'Eugh, I wouldn't sleep with someone who's dirty anyway,' but unfortunately STIs aren't that straightforward – you can't tell by looking at someone if they have an STI. In fact many infections are completely invisible.

STIs are very real and are massively on the increase in teenagers – the latest figures show that cases of chlamydia identified at Genito-Urinary Medicine (GUM) clinics in the UK rose by 76% between 1995 and 1999, with young people at the greatest risk. Plus, in 1999 cases of gonorrhoea at GUM clinics rose by 55%, with the highest rates found in women aged 16 to 19.

STIs are no laughing matter – they can lead to infertility and some can never be cured. So never take the risk, without arming yourself with the facts first. Here are some explanations of the main types of STIs:

Chlamydia: This is the most common bacterial STI in the UK. Women aged 16–24 are most at risk. Up to 90% of infected women and 25% of infected men show no symptoms, so many cases go undetected. Symptoms can be a mild increase in vaginal discharge, the need to wee more often, painful weeing, tummy ache, irregular bleeding, pain during sex and swelling or irritation of the eyes. Men should look out for white, cloudy discharge from the penis, the need to wee more often, painful weeing and swelling or irritation of the eyes. If not treated it can lead to infertility.
Treatment: Antibiotics.

Herpes: This STI is caused by the herpes simplex virus. There are two types of herpes: Type I causes coldsores on the nose and mouth and Type II causes sores in the genital area. You can pass an infection between the two types of herpes, though (i.e. a coldsore on the mouth can be passed to the genitals). Symptoms are small blisters around the mouth or genital area which can burst and leave painful sores. You might also have flu-like symptoms.
Treatment: Once you have herpes, you can't cure it – you

have to learn to live with it. There are topical treatments, but attacks can reoccur at any time.

Genital warts: This is the most common STI treated in GUM clinics, with the highest risk group being young women and men. Warts are small fleshy growths, like tiny cauliflowers, that grow on or around the genital area. They may take up to a year to appear after infection and they're not always visible – especially for women if they are inside the vagina, on the cervix or anus.
Treatment: They can be treated with ointments from the doctor and paints, freezing, or by surgical removal.

Gonorrhoea: Gonorrhoea is an STI also known as 'the clap', and teenagers are in the highest-risk category. Most women show no symptoms, but men should watch out for discharge from the penis and burning pain when weeing.
Treatment: Antibiotics.

Pubic lice: Also known as 'crabs', these are tiny grey insects that can attach themselves to pubic hair, armpit hair or the eyebrows. They cause severe itching, but are otherwise hamless.
Treatment: Lotions from the doctor.

HIV and AIDS: HIV stands for Human Immuno-deficiency Virus and someone with the virus is known as 'HIV-Positive'. The virus attacks the body's immune system, and can develop into AIDS – Acquired Immune Deficiency Syndrome. HIV symptoms are night sweats, fever, lack of energy, diarrhoea and weight loss, thrush (see pages 56–57) or herpes infections, dry skin and rashes, mouth ulcers and bleeding gums. AIDS-related symptoms which can develop are breathing problems, eyesight difficulties and infections, brain problems and cancer.

Treatment: There is no cure for HIV, but there are drug treatments available that can control it to a certain extent.

Hepatitis B: This is a viral infection of the liver. Hepatitis B is far more infectious than HIV and shows symptoms such as lack of energy and loss of appetite, fever, jaundiced (yellow) skin, yellowing of the whites of eyes, pale poo and dark wee and abdominal pain.

Treatment: NONE. But people do recover after rest, a healthy diet and not drinking.

Important note

To guard against STIs, always wear a condom, even if you are using another form of contraception such as the Pill.

Female health

There are other female-specific infections worth knowing about, that are not sexually transmitted, but very common.

Cystitis: This is a common infection or inflammation of the bladder lining, which makes it painful to wee and makes you think you have to wee all the time. It's caused by bacteria reaching the urethra, and can be the result of sex, of not drinking enough fluid to flush germs from the bladder, or of wearing tight trousers or underwear.

Treatment: Flush out your system by drinking half a litre of water, followed by a quarter of a litre every 20 minutes, until you can go to the toilet without any problems. Some people recommend drinking cranberry juice, but it must be 100% pure cranberry juice (i.e. without sugar and not from concentrate). You can also buy special formulae from the chemist.

Thrush: This is caused by an imbalance of the naturally occurring, yeast-like fungus that lives on the skin, mouth and inside the vagina. It can be caused by stress, antibiotics, tight-fitting clothes or having sex with someone. Symptoms include vaginal pain, inflammation, pain when weeing, and discharge that is a different colour, smells or itches.

Treatment: There are special creams or a pessary (a small tablet inserted inside the vagina) available from the chemist.

Q & A: Sex

The following are common questions from teenagers concerning sexual activity.

Q: *I had sex with my boyfriend, but we got so carried away, we didn't use a condom. What should I do?*

A: It isn't too late to act. You can get emergency contraception, otherwise known as the Morning After Pill, which can be taken up to 72 hours after having unprotected sex. If you are over 16 you can buy it from your local chemist. But if you are under 16, you should get it from your doctor, Family Planning or Brook clinic. It is for emergencies only, and is not safe to be used as a form of contraception.

You could also have a coil (IUD) fitted as emergency contraception. It works up to five days after having unprotected sex.

Remember, by not using any contraception you are at risk of catching STIs. You should consider getting yourself tested if you are sexually active.

Q: *I think I may have caught an STI. What do I do now?*
A: You should go to your doctor or a GUM clinic immediately and get yourself tested. Don't feel worried about going, the procedures are painless and all clinics are confidential, sympathetic and supportive. You can find your nearest GUM clinic in the phone book or Yellow Pages.

Q: *My doctor is a family friend. I'm worried he'll tell my parents if I tell him I want some contraception.*
A: Your doctor must keep your information confidential by law, so he or she cannot tell your parents. Don't feel embarrassed about getting contraception, as it's far better than having sex without it. Also you don't have to go to your doctor; you could visit a Family Planning Clinic, or Brook clinic instead. See Resources for contact numbers.

Q: *I want to have sex with my girlfriend. I feel ready, but she keeps saying no. How can I convince her?*
A: Don't try to convince her. Sex is about two people, and if one of you wants to take things further than the other, the balance is off in the relationship. If you really care about her, you'll respect her decision. If you think you

care more about having sex than you care about her, then I'm afraid you're probably not right for each other.

Q: *I got off with this boy at a party, and we had sex. I don't normally do things like that, and I thought he'd want to see me again. But he just left me upstairs and didn't talk to me again, and I haven't seen him since. I feel terrible – what should I do now?*

A: It doesn't look good with him, I'm afraid. Not everyone who has sex is looking for a relationship, and it sounds like he wasn't. You'll have to put it down to experience and try to forget it. Don't beat yourself up about it – often the only way to learn is from your mistakes. If you want a more meaningful relationship than him, you may have to be more selective next time.

Be aware: Sex

In summary, here are the main points to take away from this chapter:

1) Sex can be a wonderful experience if you're ready for it.
2) Sex and pressure don't mix. If one of you isn't ready, then neither of you is.
3) Sex under the age of 16 is illegal.
4) Contraception: Know the types. Make sure you use some.
5) Condoms protect against STIs. If you don't want to catch an infection, use a condom.

Chapter 6

Getting Home

You've had a good night out. Now you need to get home. The first thing to remember is to make arrangements about how to get home before you go out. It might not sound cool, but dodgy things can happen to people late at night, especially if you've been drinking. So ask yourself the following questions at the start of the night:

1) Who are you travelling home with?
2) How are you getting home?
3) What time will you be ready to leave?
4) Who is going to pick you up and where from?
5) Are you getting a taxi or taking public transport? Have you booked a taxi or do you know the train or bus schedule? Don't leave it to chance.

There's no shame in having your parents pick you up at the end of a night (yes, you can even forgive your mum wearing her nightie). Don't worry about looking like a loser – you're just being organised and safe. After all, you can always ask her to park the car round the corner.

Bus, train, trams, underground and taxis . . .

If you are catching public transport home, follow these simple safety rules:

- Wait on the platform, or at the bus stop, in a well-lit place.
- Keep your bag close to you at all times.

- Have the correct change ready – don't wave your wallet around.
- Sit near the driver or guard – especially late at night.
- Ask someone to meet you at the other end of your journey.

What to do if someone unwanted talks to you

Whatever type of transport you take home, there can always be a 'loony' on board – someone who is mad or drunk, and always seems to make a beeline for you. Most of the time they are harmless, but sometimes you can feel threatened by them. If this happens you can:

1) Avoid conflict, by not answering them, even when they say stupid or outrageous things to you.
2) Move seats, or carriages.
3) Talk to the driver or guard. It's better to voice your fears, even if they prove unfounded, than it is to take a risk.
4) Shout, 'I'm being followed/attacked, call the police!' if you feel really threatened. Don't be embarrassed – you need to alert others that you are in trouble.
5) If you feel really threatened, sound the emergency alarm. You can also get off and use the emergency telephone on the station, which will put you through to the transport police.
6) Call 999 or your family and friends on your mobile phone.

What to do if someone presses against you

In crowded areas, there are some sad people who get a

thrill from pressing themselves against people – either squashing their crotch against you, or sticking their hand somewhere and 'copping' a feel. If this happens to you, you can:

1) See who's doing it, or if you're not sure if it's accidental, stick your elbows out, to create room for yourself.
2) Move to another part of the bus or carriage. Get off at the next station and swap carriages if you can't push through the crowd.
3) Shout at the person. Say something like, 'Get away from me, you pervert!'
4) Ask someone for help. Pick a family group ideally, and ask if you can stick with them.
5) Tell a guard, or use the emergency phone on the station platform. The transport police will help you straight away.

Taxis

There are two types of taxis – mini-cabs and black cabs. Mini-cabs must be pre-booked from a taxi office, and black cabs can be hailed on the street. Mini-cabs are not licensed in the same way that black cabs are, so it's important that you only hail black cabs. NEVER get into a mini-cab or private car that offers you a lift in the street.

Taxi safety tips:
- Carry the number of a taxi firm you have used before or program the number into your mobile.
- Book a taxi before you go out. Ask for the driver's name and the colour and make of the car.

- When the car comes, ask the driver who he is collecting, his name and company. Don't tell him your name first.
- Always try to share a cab with a friend, and sit in the back.
- Never accept a lift from an unfamiliar car, even if they say they're a taxi. Some people drive around in their own cars trying to make extra money.
- Trust your instincts. If you feel worried, tell the driver to stop and let you out. Get out in a busy place, and phone home. If he refuses to stop, shout and wave out of the window to attract attention, or call the police on your mobile phone.

Getting home: Do's and Don'ts

Do wear a coat. It's better to seem uncool than get hypothermia. You never know when you may be outside for longer than you planned, like if your lift didn't turn up, or the bus was cancelled. And it will also draw less unwanted attention to you.

Don't walk home on your own. Try to walk in a group.

Do have shoes that you can walk/run in – take a spare pair in a bag if necessary and change into them on your way home.

Don't accept a ride from a stranger, no matter how tempting.

Do look confident.

Don't walk anywhere deserted or unlit, like parks, alleys or subways.

For more general street safety tips, see the Out and About section.

Be aware: Getting Home

In summary, here are the main points to take away from this chapter:

1) Know how you're getting home before you go out.

2) There's no shame in having mum pick you up – honestly.

3) Only take licensed cabs. No matter how tempting, don't get into an unlicensed car.

4) If you feel threatened, trust your instincts and get help immediately.

5) Walk the long way home if it's safer – don't take shortcuts through unlit or deserted areas.

Home and School

Chapter 7

Family Problems

The myth of the 'ideal family'

My name is Sophie, and I live with my brother Harry, my housewife mum Cynthia and my managing director father Malcolm. We live in a five-bedroom house in Sussex, where we spend many happy evenings singing along around the piano, or having long chats about our feelings. We all get on so well, and we last had a row in 1987.

STOP! I DON'T THINK SO! How many families do you know like that? Nowadays, it seems unusual if you have a mum and dad still together and no step-sisters or brothers. And it's downright weird if you live in a family that never has any rows or problems!

Families come in all shapes and forms, with all sorts of problems. Believe me, every family has issues to deal with, and every person feels fed up with their parents, brothers or sisters at some point.

This chapter covers some of the more serious issues we may face in the family home – how to recognise them, and how to cope with them.

Abuse in the home

Although going through your teenage years can be difficult, most of us get love and care from our families and eventually turn into happy, healthy adults (well that's the plan!). Unfortunately, some children and teenagers are hurt and neglected, or abused by family members.

ChildLine say 95% of callers reporting sexual or physical abuse know the abuser. Abusers include parents, uncles, aunts, grandparents, teachers, family friends, brothers and sisters and other children.

Q & A: Abuse

Q: *What is abuse?*

A: There are three main types of abuse:

1) Physical abuse: This is any behaviour that inflicts physical pain – ranging from punching, to slapping, to shaking, or whatever. It's when someone physically bullies and hurts you. Often people who are physically abused feel ashamed, and therefore don't tell anyone, keeping it to themselves. When physical abuse happens over a long period of time, many people develop a 'victim mentality' and in a strange way, believe they deserve the abuse, as they must have done something wrong. They haven't done anything wrong – they've just been beaten into believing this.

2) Emotional abuse: This occurs when a person is not given love, approval or acceptance and instead is blamed, shouted at or rejected. It can range from constantly being put down, to being screamed at. It can make someone feel the same way as if the abuse were physical. Many people think that emotional abuse is not that serious – after all, no one's been physically hurt. But having someone bully, torment, or even completely ignore you is just as hurtful and damaging as someone actually hitting you. Abuse bruises your mind as much as it bruises your body.

3) Sexual abuse: This occurs when someone is forced into sexual acts against their will. This is extremely traumatic to go through, and can leave you feeling confused, ashamed, guilty, and very lonely. It doesn't always have to be sex either. It can range from talking about sex, to looking at sexual pictures, to kissing, touching, or performing sex acts.

With all three types of abuse it is not limited to your parents or just in the home – it applies to anyone, from siblings and relatives to friends or strangers.

Q: *How common is abuse?*
A: It's difficult to know how many children/teenagers really are abused, because so many of us keep it a secret, but some charities say it could be as high as 1 in 10.

Q: *How can I cope with abuse?*
A: Feelings: Living with abuse is a terrible and traumatic thing to cope with. You might feel overwhelmed, isolated, angry and depressed. You might feel like it's impossible to have fun any more. Whatever the case, remember these three key facts:

1) It's NOT your fault.
2) You CAN'T control it.
3) TALKING will help.

Secrets: You might feel it's your secret to keep and that by not talking about it, it will just go away. You might also be afraid to tell anyone, because the abuser has made you promise not to, or even threatened you if you do tell. But locking it inside will not make the problem, or the abuser, go away. The pain will stay inside you and grow, causing more distress in the long-run. It will be easier to come to terms with what's happening to you if you tell someone you trust.

Effects: Abuse can have damaging long-term effects as you grow older – ranging from depression and low self-esteem to eating disorders and substance abuse. It can make it difficult to form loving relationships. That's why the first thing you should do is GET HELP (see Resources).

Remember the following key points:

1) It is not your fault. You have done nothing wrong, and should not feel guilty, even if you think you didn't resist or discourage it enough.

2) Talking will help. Even if you were told to keep it a secret, you really should tell someone straight away. It's not going to be easy, but it's just not something you can cope with on your own. Choose an adult you trust, and share your secret. Until you do this, you can't start getting your life back together. If you daren't tell a family member, you could also tell a teacher, doctor, or counsellor. Or call an organisation like the NSPCC Child Protection Helpline, Lifeline or ChildLine, who will all help you. And remember – even if another family member doesn't believe you, there will be someone who will (see Resources).

3) There is no wrong way to react to abuse. However you feel about it – from angry, to embarrassed, ashamed, confused, or even thinking it wasn't that bad, you are not responsible for what happened to you. Abuse is illegal and wrong, and you don't have to put up with it.

4) Don't panic about what may happen. The first

step is to get help, then YOU can decide what the next stages are. You don't have to worry about the police – get help for yourself first. You shouldn't keep quiet out of fear, or hope that it will go away. It is your life, and you deserve a happy and safe future.

Discussion board: Abuse

I had to make up an excuse and say I'd left my gym kit at home, so I could get out of games. I couldn't do it – the teacher and my friends would have seen the bruises on my arms when I got changed.

P-Kay, 15

It started when I was 10. My grandad said it was our special secret and I couldn't tell anyone about it. I didn't realise anything was wrong for a long time.

Natasha, 16

When my mum is not at home my step-dad always shouts at me. He calls me names and says he only puts up with me because of Mum. I tried to tell her, but she doesn't believe me.

Neil, 13

Be aware: Family Problems

In summary, here are the main points from this chapter:

1) There's no such thing as a normal family.
2) Abuse is never your fault.
3) If you live with any type of abuse, keeping quiet will not make it stop. Only speaking up and getting help will.

Chapter 8

Phone Safety

'Funny phone calls' can be seen as a bit of a joke by a lot of people – after all it's just some sad person getting their kicks from breathing heavily, isn't it? But if you get a dodgy phone call it can be very upsetting – it's like someone's intruded in your home, as you can feel in a way, by answering the telephone, you have somehow 'let them in'. You shouldn't have to live your life like in the *Scream* movies, permanently quaking every time you answer the phone – it's best to know what to do if you do get one.

Real-life story: 'I got a pervy phone call'

I was at home on my own one day when the phone rang. When I picked it up, no one spoke on the other end – all I could hear was breathing. I slammed it down, but it was really horrible. The next week it happened again, and this time this man called me by my name and asked me if I was wearing knickers. I shouted at him, and told my mum, and we got our phone number changed, but it really freaked me out.

Angela, 12

Problem phone calls

'Con calls'

One popular 'con call' is when someone rings up saying they are from a magazine or TV show, and that you have won a prize. Some parents and teenagers have even reported a caller asking to meet them somewhere. They were right to call the magazine to check if the prize was legitimate.

If you really did win a prize from a magazine, or any organisation, as well as a phone call, you would normally get a letter explaining everything on company letterhead. Then you would either receive the prize, or make other arrangements to do so. Those readers and parents who called the magazine did the right thing.

What to do: If you receive a letter saying you've won something, it's a good idea for you, or someone else, to call the phone number on the letterhead and speak to the person who wrote the letter. If you get a phone call saying you've won something, ask them to put it in writing too, so you can do the same.

Who's behind them: Often these types of calls or letters are just jokes from peers, but in some cases they could be strangers trying to get their kicks from talking to young people, or trying to meet them. If you are ever suspicious about a call like this, trust your instincts, and fetch your parents to talk to the caller.

Tips:

1) Never give out personal information on the phone if you are not sure who is calling.
2) Ask for their details and then get an adult to call back and check they are actually from the company they say they are.

Silent calls

These calls can be very annoying and upsetting – the phone rings, you get up to answer it, and there's only silence at the other end, or they simply hang up. Sometimes they keep calling back and you go through the whole thing again.

Don't panic. Before you imagine a knife-wielding maniac and call the police, there are some other possible reasons for silent calls, such as:

1) Someone could be having difficulty getting through, say, on their mobile, or from abroad.

2) A fax or computer may be dialling into your number by mistake.

3) It could even be someone who has dialled your number on their mobile by accident.

But sometimes it could be someone being stupid – like an ex-boyfriend or girlfriend you have fallen out with, or a friend you have had an argument with.

See below for action you can take.

Heavy breathing/obscene calls

As Angela told us, these types of phone calls can be very upsetting. Why anyone would want to 'huff and puff' down a phone line, or check if your underwear's matching today, we'll never know. But if you get a call like this, it's best just to hang up. And keep hanging up if they call back.

What to do: The aim of these callers is to upset and shock you, so try not to give them the satisfaction:

1) Stay calm and in control – if you show emotion then they are achieving what they want.

2) Don't get angry or shout at them, just quietly place the handset down without saying anything and leave it down. After a few minutes, put the handset back on the phone without checking to see if they are still there.

3) If they ring back, do the same thing again. And if they keep calling, a good trick is to answer the phone silently – don't say anything at all. If it's someone else they'll say, 'Hello?' But if it's the malicious caller, they'll give up as you're ruining their fun. (See Phone safety: Do's and Don'ts, pages 75–76, for more information.

4) If the calls just won't stop, and especially if they know personal information about you – your name or what you were doing today, for example – then your family should contact your phone company immediately. BT has a malicious phone call advice line (see Resources) specially set up for this. They can change your phone number, make you ex-directory, or even get the police involved to help trace the calls.

Malicious phone calls are an offence and can be prosecuted.

General phone tips

- When you answer the phone don't say your name or number – despite what you may have been taught when you were younger. It's safer to simply say 'Hello'.
- If someone says, 'Who's that?' when they call you – don't tell them straight away, ask them who they

were calling first.

- And if a caller says, 'What number's this?' ask them which number they were dialling first. Don't give out yours.

Phone safety: Do's and Don'ts

If you are worried about a phone call, put the following points into action:

Do tell your parents or another adult.

Don't panic.

Do dial 1471. If the person calling hasn't blocked their number you can find out who they are. You will most likely find it's a mistake – like they dialled the wrong number, their mobile wasn't connecting, or it could have been a child misdialling.

Don't encourage a malicious caller by saying anything to them – they want nothing more than to hear you say, 'Eugh, you pervert,' so it's best to keep silent and hang up.

Do say nothing, put the handset on the side and walk off. Firstly it's going to blow their bill sky high, and secondly you're not even listening, which ruins it for them. Then after a while, replace the handset without seeing if they are still on the line. As before, if they call back, answer the phone silently. The malicious caller will get bored – especially if you go through the whole process again and again.

Don't answer again, but use your answer phone if you have one. Switch on your machine or activate your answering service on your phone line to screen your calls. You can always pick up or call back once you hear who it is.

Do use a Caller ID machine. These are great for seeing

who's calling before you answer the phone. If you don't recognise the number, or if the screen says 'Caller Withheld' then you don't need to pick up. Innocent callers will ring again later.

Don't be embarrassed to get someone else to answer the phone. Ask an adult to answer the phone. Or, if you are female, ask a male to answer.

Do contact your phone company, if all else fails. (See BT's Malicious Calls Advice Line in Resources). They can help you in all sorts of ways – changing your number, making you ex-directory, or by putting a block on your calls.

Don't put up with it. If it's very serious and you feel threatened, or if the caller knows information about you, then your phone company can get special police investigators involved. It is an offence to make malicious calls, so they can trace the caller – wherever they are calling from.

Mobile phone safety

How many of your friends have mobile phones? Nearly everyone, probably. In fact at the time of writing, there are 3.6 million school-age mobile phone owners in the UK and it seems weird to imagine what we all did before they were invented.

But the rise of mobiles is accompanied by the rise of some problems too – from the risk of getting your phone stolen, to unwanted phone calls, or even phone bullying. Here's how to cope with these problems:

Phone security

Mugging madness: Mobile phone mugging is big business, and it's no joke – there's a mobile phone crime wave sweeping across the country. For safety tips on how to avoid being mugged for your mobile phone, see Chapter 13.

Phone scams

There are some scams around where people call or text you, asking you to phone a number, or punch a code into your phone. Don't do these – they can give other people access to your account. These people can then call from their phones at your cost.

Dodgy phone calls

The same rules apply as on your land-line. If someone starts calling and keeps silent, talks obscenely or threatens you, seek help. See earlier in this chapter for more information.

As on your land-line, NEVER give out any personal information – your name, address, school – unless you are absolutely sure you know who's calling. If someone calls you and asks who they are speaking to, ask them who they are first, before telling them.

Text safety

If you receive a text from someone you don't know, it might seem a laugh to text back, sort of like blind dating. But be careful before you start chatting away with them. Find out who they are straight away – it may seem exciting to be texting with Mr or Mrs Mystery, but it's not wise to talk intimately with any stranger – whatever the format you do it in. You might imagine they're Brad Pitt or Jennifer Aniston lookalikes on the other end, but chances are they're not. Again, don't give away any personal information about yourself.

Phone bullying

Along with the rise of mobile phones, has come the rise of mobile phone bullying – and it's just as serious and hurtful as any other form of bullying. It's widespread too – as many as one in five 14- to 16-year-olds have received text or call bullying according to a survey by research company NOP.

Phone bullying can be anything from receiving a barrage of text messages insulting you, to anonymous threatening phone calls.

Real-life story: 'I was text-terrified'

I was being bullied by this group of girls at school, and all of a sudden I started to get silent phone calls on my mobile, as well as text messages saying all sorts of things were going to happen to me. The text messages came from a website, so I couldn't trace them, but then when I started to get calls that said the same things these girls were saying, I knew it was them. In a way, it was a relief, as I thought there was someone else out there who had it in for me. I let it go on for a year, but then one day, I snapped. I was so miserable and scared, I thought it couldn't get any worse, so I told a teacher. She asked to see the messages, and it turned out I wasn't the only one. In the end the police got involved, and the girls were permanently excluded. I thought no one would be able to help me, but telling someone was the best thing I have ever done.

Samira, 14

How to stop it

Phone bullying is the same as bullying face to face and it's not on. For more help on bullying in general, see Chapter 10.

Q & A: Phone bullying

Q: *I'm being bullied by phone. What can I do?*
A: The most important thing of all is to TELL TELL TELL someone – a teacher, adult friend or relative. Also, tell your friends at school. Chances are, someone else is going through it, or has gone through it and can help you with their experience. The more people you tell, the less alone you'll feel, and the less of a burden it will seem.

Q: *But I can't do that – I'm scared.*
A: OK, telling someone may be the last thing you want to do. You might be scared, and worried what the bullies will do if you tell on them. But you really only have two choices:

1) Keep quiet and hope it will go away. Do you think it will? You'll probably have to carry on being miserable and scared for as long as they keep bully-ing you.
2) Tell someone and stand up for yourself. Yes, the bullies will go mad. Yes, you will be scared, but you have to weigh up if this risk is better than suffering any longer.

Q: *What if no one believes me?*
A: You might worry no one can help you, you might think your friends, teachers or parents won't believe you

or take you seriously, but someone will. By getting your friends involved, you may not even need to tell a teacher, as you might be able to all sort it out yourself. But if you do need further help, every school has a social behaviour policy, so they have to take bullying seriously – in whatever form. If the first teacher you speak to doesn't help, try another one, and keep trying until you find someone who will listen. Get a friend to come with you, for moral support.

Q: *How can I prove it?*
A: Save as many of the messages as you can for evidence. You need to be clear about the facts. Note when you received phone calls or messages, what day, date and time, what they said and what action, if any, you took.

Q: *But will they really stop?*
A: Don't lose heart and think nothing will change – it WILL. Bullying IS taken seriously by schools and the police. And the police can and do take action – for example, you can actually go to prison for sending malicious text messages if you cause the victim to fear for their lives.

Q: *What if I don't know who's doing it?*
A: To report a nuisance call or text, contact your phone provider's customer service line. Ask them to change your mobile number free of charge. And if it's serious, the police can track down who is calling you – text messaging can be traced, even from a website.

Be aware: Phone Safety

In summary, here are the main points to take away from this chapter:

1) Never give out personal information on the phone.

2) If you get a dodgy phone call, keep silent yourself, and spoil their fun.

3) Beware of phone scams.

4) Mobile phone bullying is as serious as any other type of bullying.

5) The best way to stop phone bullies is to tell someone.

Chapter 9

Online Safety

How many of the following statements do you agree with?

1) I use a computer regularly.	Agree ☐ Disagree ☐
2) I know more about computers and the net than my parents.	Agree ☐ Disagree ☐
3) I have visited chat rooms.	Agree ☐ Disagree ☐
4) I consider myself experienced on the net.	Agree ☐ Disagree ☐

Chances are, you've agreed with all of the above. The internet and computers have to be the number one way to separate the young from the 'crumblies'. When your dad still can't work out where the on-switch is for the video, it's not surprising that the World Wide Web's beyond him, is it?

What this means is that it's really hard for some parents to know what the internet is all about, and so they panic that you're dicing with death every time you boot up, let alone go into a chat room.

Chat facts

Chat rooms can be a real laugh, and you can make good friends through them. For every one bad experience, there are ten tales of people making new friends through the net, and being perfectly safe. But the fact remains that there are dangers to chat rooms – we've all seen the soap plots or heard scare stories of paedophiles roaming the internet searching for victims. This chapter is not meant to scare everyone going online, it's here to make sure you are clued-up to all sides of using the internet and chat rooms.

Real-life story: 'I met a pervert'

I regularly go into this teenage chat room. There are lots of people I have become mates with over the internet, as well as people I know from school on there, so I never thought much of it. But then one day I started chatting to this new guy, who was really friendly, and we swapped emails. We started emailing every day, and he sent me a picture of himself, and looked gorgeous. He lived locally and wanted to meet up, but all my friends said I shouldn't go, because it was dangerous. In the end, I arranged to meet him in a café and I went with my friend. When we got there – you guessed it – he was about 50, bald and fat. We just turned around and ran. I have never felt so disgusted in all my life.

Sophia, 14

Q & A: Online safety

Q: *How safe are chat rooms?*
A: Perfectly safe, as long as you don't give out too much information. The biggest thing about meeting people online is that you DON'T KNOW WHO THEY ARE. This is exciting in one respect, but can also be scary. Think about it – you can pretend to be any age, any sex, live anywhere or look like the complete opposite to what you say, when you start chatting to someone. How would they know? So what makes you think they are not doing the same to you? I bet every time a girl says her age online, the bloke talking to her says he's older. Right?

That's the trick. It's not a problem if you leave it at that, and don't take it any further, but when you start believing the other person and getting interested in them, then you should be cautious.

Q: *What should I say then?*
A: Basically, have fun, and say whatever you like, as long as it's NOT personal information. Don't tell them your name, address, telephone number or where you work or go to school. You have no way of knowing who they are or what they are like.

Q: *Should I chat off-line?*
A: If you want to give someone your email address, or chat in real time, that's up to you – but again, don't give them any more personal information than that. It's not safe to give out your phone number or tell someone your address.

Q: *My online friend sent me a picture of herself. How do I know it's really her?*
A: Well you don't know, do you? It could be a photo of anyone – some people send pictures of their friends or relatives instead, or even cut pictures out of magazines, or download them from other sites. You can usually rumble this, though, by looking at how professional the photo appears. Unless they really are a mega-star, not many people have a professional photographer, make-up artist and stylist on hand for their holiday snaps, do they? The fact is, you have no real way of knowing it is them. Again, don't trust anyone until you can verify details about them.

Q: *I'd like to meet up with a chat-room friend. Can I?*
A: Yes, you can, but you have to be careful. Never meet anyone on your own. Two things to remember are:

1) Take someone: Always take an adult or friend. You can never be sure until you get there, so what's the deal with feeling stupid because your mum's in tow? It's better to meet like that and feel secure, than take risks. After all, if your new friend is a good friend, then they will understand your caution and should be doing the same thing themselves. Your mum or friend can always leave you to it once they have checked them out, and then come back later.
2) Meet in public: Always meet in a public place, somewhere that you are familiar with. Tell someone where you will be at all times, and don't go off anywhere on your own with the person you are meeting – especially in their car or to their house.

Q: *What if I get there and don't like them, or they weren't who they said they were?*
A: Then turn around and walk away. Embarrassing or rude? – Yes. But worth it? – Definitely. If you thought you were meeting a boy or girl, for example, and it turned out to be a much older man – no matter how nice he seems to be, or how sorry you feel for him, leave immediately. It's better to be rude than put yourself in danger.

Q: *When I was online this person started saying really dirty things to me, and I didn't know what to do. What should I do in the future?*
A: First, try to remember their name. Then get out of the site. Next, tell your parents or an adult if anything online

makes you feel uncomfortable. The internet has the same laws as the rest of the world, so if someone makes a nuisance of themselves, they can be prosecuted.

Safe-surfing checklist

If in doubt, follow these rules set by AOL Kids:

1) Never tell anyone your last name, address or phone number, or where you go to school.
2) Tell someone – parents, teachers or adults – if anything online makes you feel uncomfortable.
3) Never meet up with a friend off-line, unless an adult is with you. You can not be sure they are who they say they are.
4) Make sure you know where files are from before you download them. They could contain viruses.
5) Don't send chain emails or nasty messages. If you get any, show your parents, and don't send them on (see below).

For more advice check out www.chatdanger.com

Chain emails

Once upon a time, what seems a million years ago, these used to be chain letters – a letter posted to you saying that something terrible would happen or you would get bad luck if you didn't send on 10 copies in one day, or whatever. Now, technology's moved on to chain emails.

The good: These can be from charities saying they'll donate money if you send them on or click a link, or they could be something like petitions about something you want to change. These are fine, and perfectly safe. But it's still worth looking closely – some can be fake.

The annoying: Then you get on someone's email list and start receiving 10,000 corny jokes from round the world, or games and quizzes you can play to discover some truth about yourself. Annoying yes, dangerous, no.

The scams: You might get an email asking you to add your name on to the bottom and some internet provider or big company will send you money or free gifts. Does it work? What do you reckon?

The superstitious: And then there are the emails saying that if you send the email on you will have good friends, good luck or whatever for the rest of your life and if you don't, some terrible thing will happen to you. This is nonsense, of course.

Bin 'em: Don't ever feel worried about any chain email – even if it says something bad's going to happen if you break the chain, or you won't be a true friend, lucky in love or win the lottery — it's all waffle, believe me. Just bin the emails and don't think another thing about them. They are just set up by people with too much time!

Scared?: Of course, if you feel really worried about a chain email, show it to a friend, parent or teacher, as you never want to receive anything threatening.

Be aware: Online Safety

In summary, here are the main points to take away from this chapter:

1) Not all chat rooms are dodgy.
2) Don't give out personal information online.
3) You don't know if someone online is telling the truth, or

if their photo is really of them.
4) If you meet someone off-line, take a friend or adult with you.
5) Chain emails are at best a laugh, at worst, pointless. If in doubt, bin them!

Chapter 10

Bullying

Discussion board: Bullying

The following are just a few thoughts and opinions about bullying. What do you think?

'They got excluded'

I started a new school last year, and when I got there this group of boys from another form started picking on me. They'd push me around, and ask me for money, and I tried to stand up for myself but it got worse and worse until they ended up beating me up. So then I started bunking off and wandering round town instead of going to school. Eventually I was reported and I had to tell my dad what was going on. He went straight to the school and they took it more seriously than I thought – they excluded two of the boys for two weeks and one permanently. It did get better after that.

Andrew, 14

'Stand up'

I think people get bullied because they aren't strong enough. This boy picked on me, and I fought back. He never did it again, and neither did anyone else.

Simon, 16

'Nothing happened'

I've been bullied for three years by three girls in the year above. They follow me home and threaten me. My parents said I should stand up for myself, but eventually they phoned the school and one of the girls got excluded. But the others carried on, and then the first girl got let back into school anyway – it's still happening and it's making my life a misery.

Helen, 14

'We drove her out of school'

Me and my mates picked on this girl in our first year. She smelt of BO, so every day we cut loads of ads for soap and deodorant out of magazines and put them in her locker. She changed schools in the end. We thought it was a laugh at the time, but looking back, I suppose we could have been done for bullying.

Emma, 17

Bullying: The telly theory

If you believe the soaps, the bully always gets it in the end. Beefy Baxter the Bully rules by fear, nicking money and food off the poor little first-years. They hatch some cunning plans to try to get him back, but nothing works, until one day, they tell the kindly metalwork teacher, who's shocked and appalled, and the school finally excludes him. And everyone lives happily ever after.

Bullying: The truth

Except it doesn't work like this in real life, does it? Bullying is always far more complicated – sometimes teachers don't believe you, sometimes your parents just tell you to stand up for yourself, sometimes the bully gets away with it. Or even worse, sometimes the bully gets let back into school again after they've been excluded, and so is even more determined to get you.

This book can't guarantee that you'll never get bullied, but it can give you some pointers on what to do if you are.

The law

It's the law that every school has an anti-bullying policy. The Department for Education and Skills states: 'Each school should have a clear school behaviour policy. It should make clear the boundaries of what is acceptable, the hierarchy of sanctions, arrangements for their consistent and fair application and a linked system of rewards for good behaviour. It should promote respect for others, intolerance of bullying and harassment, the importance of self-discipline and the difference between "right and wrong".' They also say the anti-bullying measures your head teacher puts into place should be publicised to you and your parents.

Note: Plus there's good news for people like Helen – the government is backing plans to stop pupils appealing against exclusions for bullying and getting back into the same schools as their victims.

Q & A: Bullying

Q: *So what is bullying?*
A: It's important to realise that bullying doesn't just mean being physically attacked – it can be using snide remarks, stealing, sending text messages (see Chapter 8), intimidation, making someone fearful, feel degraded, or do things they don't want to do. It can mean different things to different people – from name-calling, teasing, hitting, stealing and rumour-mongering, to saying nasty

things, ignoring you or forcing you to hand over money or possessions.

Q: *Why do people bully?*
A: Although you might not have any sympathy for them, bullies have problems – maybe they don't fit in at school, or maybe they have issues at home. They could even be bullied themselves – at home or school. They are clearly not happy with themselves, and by having power over someone else it makes them feel better. Things you should know about bullies are:

1) It's not about you. Obviously it's hard not to take it personally, but remember that the bully doesn't have something against you above anyone else. They 're just exercising control to make themselves feel better and more powerful.

2) They may not know they're doing anything wrong. Sometimes people start teasing someone. For example, a group of friends start teasing someone in their class for being fat. They give them a name, like 'Flump' or 'Tellytubby' and then it sticks, and every time they see that person, they shout things at them. 'Tellytubby' goes home and cries – the others don't even know they're bullying. They think they're just having a laugh.

3) Bullies have their own problems. They might be bullied themselves, have problems at home, or feel insecure and inadequate.

Real-life story: 'I was a bully'

I was 16, and about to sit my GCSEs. Thinking about it now, I can see I was scared but I didn't know that at the time. I wasn't doing very well at school, my dad left my mum, and she was drinking a lot, so I didn't spend much time at home. So I took it all out on this boy for a year. I did fail my exams, but I left school and did re-takes at college. I've never bullied anyone else.

Nathan, 18

What to do if you get bullied

1) Remember it's not your fault – you are not to blame, and you don't deserve to be bullied. It's the bully's problem, but it's also become yours now, so you should get help to stop it.

2) Talk. Try talking it over with a friend or sibling. See what they say, and what you can do together.

3) Get advice. Some schools have student counsellors who can help people who've been bullied. They might have been through it themselves, and can give you some tips on how to cope. You could also try calling some helplines or visiting bullying websites, which are also helpful (see Resources).

4) Tell someone. Tell a teacher you trust. Or discuss it with your parents and ask them to visit the school. This will seem hard, but if you really want the bullying to stop, it may be your best chance.

5) Keep a diary of what is happening. Stick to the facts, like showing the dates and times they bullied you, or what they did to you, or how you reacted.

Tips

A website set up by fellow pupils called Pupiline (www.pupiline.co.uk) offers practical solutions to being bullied. They suggest you:

- Ignore the attackers (they want to think they're hurting you, so by shutting them out, they should get bored).
- Defend yourself *only* if necessary.
- Stay in a group as much as possible.
- Be firm. Shout 'NO', loudly, to get attention and help.
- Talk to other people who have been bullied, as they will know what to do.
- Be confident, stand up for yourself, and don't be afraid to show your individuality. If someone teases you, answer back, but don't get into a slanging match.
- Don't let anyone fob you off with the idea that your problems are not as significant as anyone else's. Far from it – everyone counts!

Are you a bully?

If you are bullying someone, or have bullied in the past, it is a good idea to start talking about it and get some help. Think about who would best listen to you and help you – your parents, a teacher you trust, or even a helpline like Kidscape (see Resources). You may feel stupid admitting it, but this would be the bravest thing you could do, and would make a big difference to the rest of your life.

Helping a friend: Do's and Don'ts

Do you know someone who is being bullied? Maybe they're your friend, or maybe they're just in your class. There *is* something you can do about it. Don't think that you can't make a difference and ignore bullying, or you'll let the bullies win. Here are a few Do's and Don'ts that can make a difference:

Don't rush over and confront the bullies. You may get hurt or involved in the problems personally.

Do let a teacher or adult know what's happening.

Don't ignore it – if you see something happening, you should speak up.

Do try to be a friend to the person being bullied.

Don't join in.

Do try to be nice to the bully. Odd as this may sound, friendship can sometimes stop the bully.

Don't try to sort it all out yourself. You may not be able to fix it alone – so it's a good idea to get some help from an adult.

Getting your school to say no to bullying

Your school has a duty to stop bullying, but some do this more than others. If you want to make a difference at your school, ChildLine suggest you try these tips to make your school even safer:

1) Get everyone you can in the school involved to stop bullying – the teachers, pupils, dinner ladies and playground assistants or support staff.

2) Discover how much bullying takes place in your school by organising a questionnaire with a teacher's help, that you then give to all pupils to fill out anonymously, and ask them to put in a locked box (so no one can read anyone else's answers). You can then write up a report for everyone to read.

3) Make sure your school has a good selection of anti-bullying books in the library. Suggest the school runs an anti-bullying week.

4) Ask the teachers for assemblies and class discussions about bullying – you can make posters, write stories, perform plays . . .

5) Make sure you feel safe in the playground, and that there are enough supervisors around.

6) A lot of schools set up 'peer counselling' schemes, where older pupils advise younger ones and help with bullying problems. If your school does not have this, talk to a teacher about setting one up.

For more information on how to learn more about bullying or where to get help, see Resources.

Be aware: Bullying

In summary, here are the main points to take away from this chapter:

1) Every school has to have an anti-bullying policy, by law.

2) Bullying can take many forms – it doesn't just mean physical harm.

3) The bully doesn't think about you personally.

4) If you're being bullied, talk to someone you trust.

5) You can stop bullying and make a difference.

Chapter 11

Sexual Harassment

Q & A: Sexual harassment

Q: *What is sexual harassment?*
A: Sexual harassment occurs when a sexual encounter is totally unwanted, and is one that makes you feel upset, afraid and unhappy. It can be anything from personal comments, to touching, or asking for sexual favours, or even trading sex for better grades or a promotion at work.

Q: *Is it taken seriously?*
A: Very much so – it's illegal under the Sex Discrimination Act and in some cases it is a criminal offence, so people can go to prison for it. The Equal Opportunities Commission says, 'Sexual harassment, far from being "just a bit of fun" as some people try to claim, makes people's lives a misery, affecting their confidence and their health, as well as their performance at work.'

Q: *Can you be sexually harassed by someone your own age? At my school there are these boys who follow me and my friend Emily around. They say things about her boobs, and then they do things like push against us from behind and pretend to be having sex with us. Once they even shouted, 'I'll come round your house and rape you.' Is this sexual harassment?*
A: Yes. Sexual harassment can be done by anyone of either sex, at any age. Emily's experience does count as sexual harassment, so the best thing she and her friend

could do is report boys to a teacher, so they don't get away with it any more.

Q: *Can men be sexually harassed?*
A: Yes. You may think that sexual harassment is just a female problem, and that it can't happen to boys. But if a girl harasses a boy about his sexuality, uses harmful sexual references or physically harasses him, then it counts just the same, and he can take action. You can also be sexually harassed by someone of the same sex.

Q: *What exactly counts as sexual harassment?*
A: According to the Equal Opportunities Commission it is any unwelcome physical, verbal or non-verbal conduct of a sexual nature such as:

- comments on the way you look
- indecent remarks
- questions or comments on your sex life
- requests for sexual favours
- demands from someone of the opposite sex or your own sex
- any conduct that creates an intimidating, hostile, or humiliating working environment for you on the grounds of your sex.

Q: *What should I do if someone says a personal comment to me? I have auburn hair, and last week in a swimming lesson, some boys in my class asked me if I have ginger pubes, as they saw my underarm hair. It was really embarrassing and I was dead upset. But the sports teacher just laughed. I didn't like it, it made me feel creepy.*
A: This sort of banter may well have been meant as

'harmless' by the boys, or the teacher. People have different tolerance levels, so some might not be bothered by those sorts of comments, whereas others could get very upset. Either way, if someone makes personal remarks to you, the best thing to do is speak up. (How annoying is it when you go bright red, shuffle off, and then think up a cutting comeback half an hour later?) You could say something like this:

To a student:

- 'Go away and talk to me when you've grown up.'
- 'I would laugh if I thought that was funny.'
- 'Don't talk to me like that.'
- 'Shame you don't put those powers of observation to use in your exams.'
- 'I could ask you the same question, but hmm, by the look of it, I'll have to wait a few years.'

And if they continue to make personal remarks to you, say:

- 'Look, say something like that again, and you'll be saying it to the Head.'
- 'I don't care what you say to me, but our Head of Year might.'

Talk to your mates about it, and try to stay in a group as much as you can. Then all of you can answer back, or report them if needs be.

To a teacher:

- 'You shouldn't say things like that.'
- 'I can't believe you said that.'
- 'Don't talk to me like that.'
- 'That comment made me feel uncomfortable.'

Or really shock them by saying: 'I don't think that's an

appropriate way to talk to your pupils, Sir/Miss.'

If that doesn't stop the comments, the best thing to do is talk to another teacher about it right away.

Q: *What if someone says something really disgusting?*
A: If anyone says something very offensive, then you have to take it really seriously. You don't have to cause a big scene. You could rope in a friend to help you, if you like, or even get your parents to deal with it. Pick a teacher you trust, and tell them what's happened. As with bullying, it's important to keep a record of the facts.

Q: *But what if the teacher doesn't believe me?*
A: You're right – telling a teacher doesn't always sort it out straight away, especially if they try to dismiss it and say you're over-reacting. But like bullying, the only way to stop it happening any more, is to keep talking. Work out who's best to talk to, and who you get on well with. It could be your parents, or it could be another teacher that doesn't even teach you, but who is nice or sympathetic.

Q: *What should you do if someone touches you up, or gropes you?*
A: When you know it wasn't an accident – that is, when someone squeezes, feels, pats, gropes or touches you, especially on your bum, boobs or crotch – then it should be taken very seriously. If anyone, a pupil or a teacher touches you this way, don't stand for it, even if they think it's a joke. Shout something like, 'What are you

doing? Stop it!' very loudly, push them off, tell them you are going to report them and seek help immediately.

Q: *Why can't teachers go out with pupils?*
A: First, it's a misuse of the teacher's position, and second it's illegal. The teacher is meant to guide you through school and into adulthood. Because they are much older than you, and telling you what to do, and how to learn, they have a lot of power over you. So if they suddenly started dating you, they would have more power than you, and the relationship would be one-sided.

It's not to say it never happens. You read stories in the papers of female teachers shacking up with their male pupils, or male teachers running off with girls. They all lose their jobs, and many go to jail.

However much you think you fancy your teacher, (eugh, with some of them it doesn't bear thinking about!) or however flattering someone's attention is, the odds are well stacked against it ever working out, for either of you. And that's why if a teacher started making moves on you, the best thing you could do is tell someone and stop them straight away.

Q: *What about those students who make up stories about their teachers?*
A: Sexual harassment is always taken very seriously when reported – especially between pupils and teachers. Unfortunately, a small number of pupils sometimes make false claims against a teacher, knowing that it will get them in serious trouble, and probably fired. It's a really

malicious thing to do. No matter how much you dislike someone, ruining their life is not the answer.

What do you think?

What do you count as sexual harassment?

My friend and I were walking down the road, when a man in a white van leant out the window and whistled. He shouted, 'Oi, gorgeous – nice legs!' and drove off. I laughed and walked on, but my friend said that was sexual harassment and people shouldn't be allowed to say things like that. Who's right?

Karene, 16

What do you think?

1) It's no big deal, and it's harmless.
2) People should be stopped from saying things like that in public.
3) It's OK sometimes if you're feeling happy, but if you'd just had some bad news, for example, you wouldn't really appreciate it.

There is no one right answer to this – it depends on your viewpoint, and how the comment was said. That's why it's difficult to measure – what one person may find offensive, another may not.

Be aware: Sexual Harassment

In summary, here are the main points to take away from this chapter:

1) Sexual harassment is illegal.
2) It's not just about women – men and women can be sexually harassed, by either sex.

3) People have different tolerance levels to harassment.

4) Personal comments count as sexual harassment.

5) If someone sexually harasses you at school, staying silent is the worst thing you can do.

Out and About

Chapter 12

Beat the Bag Snatchers

Quiz: How streetwise are you?

1) In your backpack, you usually keep your wallet:
a) In an outside pocket, so you can find it easily.
b) Inside the main compartment.
c) Anywhere you bung it.

2) In a busy street, if you didn't have a bag, you'd keep your wallet:
a) In your back pocket.
b) In an inside pocket.
c) In your hand.

3) At a party, in a bar or a club, you:
a) Put your bag or coat on the pile with everyone else's.
b) Put your coat in the cloakroom. You don't care if it costs.
c) Hold your coat and bag until you get fed up with it, then put it somewhere you can see it.

4) In a cafe, you'd:
a) Put your bag on the floor by your feet.
b) Put your bag on the table top.
c) Put your bag anywhere you feel like.

5) At the cashpoint, someone's standing really close to you. You:

a) Stand in front of the display so they can't see your PIN number.
b) Walk off to another cashpoint.
c) Ask them to stand back a bit.

How did you score?

Mostly A's: Street Defeat – Oh dear, when it comes to being streetsmart, you need a bit of help. You may as well make a hat out of all your money and wear it, you make that many safety boobs when you're out. But don't worry, luckily you're reading this book, and it could save you some serious hassle in the future.

Mostly B's – Street Savvy: Get you – old wise one. Someone has their head on their shoulders, and is a bit of an eagle-eye when it comes to looking after their cash and possessions. Well done – the more aware you are, the better.

Mostly C's: Street Beat – In terms of street awareness, you're a midfielder. You're on the ball sometimes, but other times you could easily let someone else score, with your bag, or wallet. So brush up on your safety skills and you'll stop the thieves from striking any day.

Real-life story: 'My cashpoint nightmare'

I met my friend at about 7pm in town to go to the cinema. I needed to get some money from the cashpoint, and as we walked up to it, we were chatting away. There was a man behind us, and my friend said to me, 'Put your purse away, that man is really close,' so I got my money out quickly and we walked off to the cinema. Just before we turned into the entrance, the same man barged between us, and pushed past me. He rushed off and the next thing I knew, my bag had been unzipped and my purse was gone, with my bank card in it and all my money. I was really upset and rang the bank and cancelled the card straight away. A few days later I was told that he must have memorised my PIN number, pickpocketed me, and then gone back to the cashpoint, because he had taken out £100 from my account. I did get most of the money back from the bank, but it took ages, and I lost the £30 I had just taken out, completely.

Jordan, 17

When you are out and about, even in the daytime, you can never be too aware of your surroundings. Nearly everyone reading this will know someone who has had their bag stolen, or wallet pinched. So it pays to be careful when you are out in any public places – either shopping, going for a drink, or going to a club. This chapter shows you how to keep your possessions safe at all times:

Getting money from the cashpoint

As Jordan found out, people are getting clever at cashpoint crimes. Not only can people look over your shoulder to read your PIN number, but they can also use mobile phones to note down your number, or even use cards to scan your number after you've used the machine.

Safety tips:

    1) It's best to get money out in the daytime, not at night.

    2) Ideally get cash out when someone else is with you.

3) Look around. If you see anyone loitering too close to the cash machine, don't take any money out. Walk away to another machine.

4) Stand in the way of the person behind you, so they can't see over your shoulder at the number you are typing in.

5) Put your money in your wallet, and your wallet in your bag before walking away. Don't walk off with the cash or wallet in your hand, as someone could easily snatch it.

6) Try not to get distracted – don't start chatting to someone else while you get money out.

Pickpockets

Another risk when you are out is pickpockets and thieves. Unfortunately they are part and parcel of life now – especially in big cities. A thief only needs a minute to run off with your valuables and sadly you can never be too careful when it comes to pickpockets. They are often very skilled and so lightning quick that you have no idea what has happened, until you look for your stuff later.

The Home Office issue the following checklist:

Safety tips:

1) Don't carry your wallet in a pocket on the outside of your bag (especially outside-pockets of a back-pack) – these are easy to unzip and remove in a busy street.

2) Carry your wallet in an inside pocket, ideally one that does up. Don't carry it in your back pocket. If someone bumps into you in a crowd, check to see if you still have your wallet.

3) In a crowd, turn the clasp or zip of your bag to face you, and keep the bag as close as possible to you.

4) Try not to carry a lot of cash.

5) If your credit or bank card is stolen, call the card company immediately.

6) Don't keep your PIN number with your cash card. Memorise it, and don't tell your friends your number.

Bag snatchers

No matter how alert you think you are, bag snatchers can still find away of luring away your bag, even if you just look away for a second. In busy places, they can do all sorts of ruses like hook your bag strap from under your feet and drag it away, or swap your bag for an empty one without you noticing. You might think keeping your bag close to you at all times is going over the top, but it's not as much of a pain as losing it.

Safety tips:

a) Avoid bags that you carry in your hand, as these are easy to snatch. Shoulder bags, or ones with straps across your body are best.

b) Never let your bag out of your sight. Don't dump it on the floor away from you – even if it is heavy. And don't put it down by the side of your chair where you can't see it, as someone can drag it away without you noticing.

c) If you must put your bag on the floor, put your feet either side of it.

d) Don't leave your bag on view in a car, even when

you're inside, as a thief could reach in and take it when you're stopped at lights.

e) Keep your house keys in your pocket – not in your bag.

f) Don't leave bags and coats in a corner of the room when in a bar, club or party, as someone can easily go through them. If you leave your coat on a peg, make sure you keep an eye on it. It's better in a cloakroom, or with you.

Note: This chapter covers cashpoint safety, pickpockets and bag thieves. For violent bag snatching and mugging, see Chapter 13.

Be aware: Beat the Bag Snatchers

In summary, here are the main points to take away from this chapter:

1) Never carry your wallet in your back pocket, in a busy place.

2) Be wary of other people at cashpoints.

3) Keep your wallet inside your bag, and the bag close to your body.

4) If you put your bag on the floor, put your feet either side of it.

5) Don't keep your PIN number with your card.

Chapter 13

Mugging and Carjacking

Mobile madness

Fact: Mobile phone mugging is big business, and it's no joke – there's a mobile crime wave sweeping across the country.

Fact: Since 1995 mobile phone robberies have increased by 190%.

Fact: Up to half a million people aged between 11 and 15 had their mobile phones stolen in 2000, according to the Home Office.

Fact: Teenagers are at the highest risk of mobile phone theft – they are five times more likely to be mugged than adults. Most mobile muggings are by gangs of teenage boys.

Discussion board: Mobile mugging

'People write it off'

I don't think mobile-phone theft is taken seriously enough. I was mugged for my phone, and when we called the police, they said it happens all the time and there's not much they can do about it.'

Hedley, 16

'They abused me'

I was sitting on a wall with my friend when these two boys came over to us. They started calling me names, saying, 'Go home, Paki' and stuff like that. Then they said if I didn't give them my phone they'd put a brick through my window, so I had to give it to them.

Mhera, 14

'I don't have a phone any more'
I had three mobile phones stolen off me in a row. Every time it happened when I was going home on the bus, and a different gang picked on me or punched me until I gave in. I don't use one now. There's just no point.

Raz, 15

How to avoid mobile mugging
To keep you and your mobile phone safe, stick to the following rules:

1) Don't walk around with your mobile in your hand.

2) Try not to have your phone on display, or clipped on to you. It's easy for would-be robbers to snatch it off you.

3) Keep your phone inside your bag, or in an inside pocket – not in a pocket that can be easily unzipped.

4) Don't make loud phone calls in public as you walk along, especially at night.

5) Try to limit making phone calls or sending text messages to areas you feel safe in.

6) Lock your phone in the glove box or boot if you leave it in a car.

7) Don't make calls as soon as you leave a train or tube station, as thieves love to hang around these busy areas.

8) If you see someone approaching you, or feel wary of a crowd of teenagers, then trust your instincts.

Keep your phone out of sight, and walk away.

Tips:

1) Consider taking out insurance on your mobile phone. It may seem a bit pricey, but it might cost less than replacing it. Or, ask your parents to extend their home insurance to cover your phone.

2) Switch your phone on using the PIN number access feature.

3) Register your phone with your supplier when you start using it. They can put a bar on the number if you report it stolen.

4) Consider security marking your phone with your postcode. Some phone shops offer this for free. Or go to your local police station, as they run schemes to code phones.

5) Register your phone with the Mobile Equipment National Database (08707 451141) to increase your chance of getting it back if it is stolen.

What to do if you get mobile-mugged

1) If someone threatens you for your mobile, especially if they have a weapon, then it's better to give them your mobile than risk getting injured.

2) Call your network provider to report it stolen and they will put a bar on your SIM card.

3) Report it to the police. When you get home, tell your parents and they can call the police to report it stolen.

Real-life story: 'I was steamed at a bus stop'

I was coming out of a burger bar with my friend, when this gang of boys ran over to us and 'steamed' us – they barged into us, pushed me into this bus shelter, hit me and knocked me down. Then they ripped off my leather jacket, the chain round my neck, my watch, rings and wallet. My friend ran away, trying to save himself. I just sat there, in the winter, in my T-shirt with no money – I didn't know how I was going to get home. In the end my friend came back and helped me.

Anthony, 14

There are 200,000 violent muggings a year in London. A quarter of all mugging victims are teenage boys aged 14 to 17. Being mugged is a traumatic experience – physically and emotionally. Like for Anthony, it can really shake you up. You're busy going about your everyday life one minute, and the next, 'bam!' you've had things wrenched off you, or you've been hurt. Plus you've probably lost something of value.

What is a mugging?

Basically it's any way of stealing something from you by force. Mugging can mean:

- being attacked by a group of people, or just one person
- being threatened with weapons, or words
- someone using physical force to beat you up, or knock you down
- extreme bullying – threatening and then forcing you to give up your possessions
- running past and grabbing your bag

How to avoid being mugged: Do's and Don'ts

Do be aware of what's going on around you, when you walk down the street.

Don't walk in deserted or dark areas, like alleyways, unlit carparks or parks.

Do use well-lit, busy roads with other people on them.

Don't talk to someone on your phone as you walk.

Do look confident.

Don't wear headphones.

Do keep all valuables out of sight.

Don't take risks. If you feel scared, listen to your feelings. Go the long way home, if it's the safest way.

Do avoid gangs of people – especially teenage boys. Try not to walk right through them or past them. Go another way home or cross over the road if you need to.

See the safety tips, pages 116–117, for more advice.

What to do if you are mugged

1) To fight or not to fight? Only you will know if it is a good idea to fight back. It depends on the situation. Some people manage to fight off the attacker and keep their possessions. Other people get hurt far worse by trying to hold on to their stuff. There's no right or wrong answer, but it's probably safer just to let your stuff go. It's only material possessions and it's much better to lose that than to get seriously hurt.

2) Make sure you're safe. Are you hurt? Do you need help? If so, try to attract a passer-by (preferably a family or couple) to help you. Get them to call your parents, or 999.

3) Get medical help. If you're injured, a passer-by should be able to call an ambulance for you, and help will be on the way.

4) Talk to the police. Your parents can call the police and ask them to talk to you. You shouldn't feel scared. Try your best to remember everything about what happened, such as a description of the mugger's face and clothes.

5) Don't be embarrassed. Being mugged is not your fault. It doesn't make you look weedy, and there's no need to feel ashamed. You might feel shaken up for some time after, and this is perfectly normal. Don't fight your feelings – you've had a shock and need to repair yourself mentally and physically.

6) See if you're insured. With any loss of possessions, home insurance sometimes covers your loss even if you are away from home. If you are on holiday, your holiday insurance should cover you as well.

General 'out and about' safety tips

- **Pre-plan.** Always let someone know where you are and what time you will arrive.
- **Wear the right clothes.** Make sure you are comfortably dressed for wherever you are going and have shoes you can walk or run in. Although you may not want to take a coat on a night out, it is much safer to be covered up and warm on the way there and back. You will draw less attention to yourself and cover any jewellery or fancy clothes and you will also be warmer on the way home, should you have to wait longer than planned outside.
- **Look confident.** If it looks like you know where you're going, and what you are doing, you are less likely to get hassled.

- **Always walk in well-lit areas.** Avoid anywhere deserted or unlit, like alleys or subways and don't walk through parks at night.
- **Don't walk alone.** Wherever you can, walk in pairs or with a group.
- **Walk towards oncoming traffic.** This makes you more visible, and you'll avoid kerbcrawlers.
- **Walk in the centre of the pavement.** This avoids getting too close to parked cars or doorways where someone could be lurking.
- **Hide valuables.** Don't flaunt your wealth – cover up your jewellery and keep your mobile phone hidden.
- **Watch the stopped cars.** Avoid passing stationery cars with engines running and people in them. Cross to the other side of the road if necessary.
- **Don't wear headphones.** You need to hear what's going on – if you wear a walkman, discman or MP3 player, for example, it'll be difficult to hear someone approach you.
- **Trust your instincts.** If you feel endangered in any way, run, and make straight for a public place like a garage or a shop, where you can call for help.

Carjacking

In the last few years a new term has come into our culture – carjacking. Before, it was the kind of crime you saw only in movies, but now there are few of us who haven't heard of this crime.

Q & A: Carjacking

Q: *What is carjacking?*
A: Carjacking is when someone (a carjacker) steals a car,

scooter or motorbike from under your nose. Someone gets you out of your vehicle, jumps in and drives off. It is most likely to happen in big cities. In 2001 there were 1,200 carjackings in London.

Q: *How do they do it?*
A: Carjackers use tactics like:
- 'Bumping' into you in a pretend accident, to get you out of the car before they jump in.
- Jumping into your car when you are stopped at traffic lights and forcing you out.
- Watching as you park or unlock your car, only to drag you out of the way and steal it.
- Dragging you right off your scooter and stealing it.
- Threatening you, using physical force or weapons, so you give up your car keys.

Q: *Why do people do it?*
A: The more high-tech our cars get, the more secure they become. Virtually all new cars have immobilisers and alarms, wheel locks or bars. So if you're Mr Car Thief, you're going to be a bit miffed that you've spent, say 10 seconds, picking a lock, only to find you can't drive off anywhere. There must be an easier way – wait until someone's driving a car, drag them out of their seat, slip in yourself, and presto, drive off. Experts say most car-jackings are done by organised gangs.

Q: *Do people ever get their cars back?*
A: Yes. Up to 80% of stolen cars are recovered every year.

Q: *How can you guard against carjacking?*
A: There are lots of things you can do to safeguard yourself, your friends and your family. Even if you haven't passed your driving test, these tips are worth knowing as a passenger:

1) Don't leave anything valuable on the car seat, even when driving. Hide phones and laptops especially.

2) Always lock your doors in cities, even when you are just driving along.

3) Make it look like you know where you're going, and only stop to look at a map in a safe area.

4) Don't wind your windows down far enough to allow someone to reach in while you are stopped in traffic.

5) Leave a small gap between your car and the one in front, so you always have room to drive away.

6) If someone rams you and you don't think it's an accident, don't get out of the car. Drive off and don't stop until you get to a service station or somewhere busy. Call 999, and try to remember the other car's number plate.

7) If you think you are being followed, try to alert others by flashing your lights or sounding your horn. Make as much noise as possible. If you can, keep driving until you arrive at a busy place.

8) Have your keys ready when you approach your car.

9) Try to always park in a well-lit, busy place. Look around before you get out of the car.

10) The AA recommends drivers fit tracking devices to their vehicles. Then if the the car is stolen, the police can find and recover the car to catch the thief.

Be aware: Mugging and Carjacking

In summary, here are the main points to take away from this chapter:

1) Keep your mobile phone out of sight as much as possible.
2) Think about getting your mobile security marked.
3) If someone mugs you, it's better to let your possessions go than get hurt.
4) Avoid walking past gangs of boys.
5) Keep your car doors locked when driving in busy cities.

Chapter 14

Aggression and Assault

Help! It's mad out there!

Sometimes it's hard to mind your own business. Especially when someone else with a problem is out looking for a fight. Have you ever been shouted at in the street? Have you ever been called names? Has someone ever picked a fight with you? Have you ever been beaten up? Chances are something like this has happened to you, or someone you know. In fact, according to a recent survey by the Joseph Rowntree Foundation, one quarter of 15- to 16-year-old boys have carried a weapon in the past year and 19% of them have attacked someone intending to hurt them. Scary.

Staying home for the rest of your life is not an option, neither is hiring an army tank to ferry you about town. The best way to combat other people's aggression is to avoid it and plan what to do ahead of time. Simply read the following scenarios and think about what you would do.

What would you do if . . .

You're a 15-year-old girl, walking into town. You pass some scaffolders who whistle and shout, 'Nice tits, darling!' You:

a) walk on and ignore them.

b) shout back, 'Nice willy, mate.'

c) feel really upset, and go home.

We discussed this briefly in Chapter 11. How would this comment make you feel? Some girls laugh it off, others feel offended. However you feel, the best approach is to walk off and make no response – sometimes shouting back inflames the situation.

You are out with your friends when someone points and calls you a black bastard. It's not the first time you've received racist remarks. You:
a) are very upset, but keep quiet and try to carry on as normal.
b) scream at them that they are racist idiots.
c) get your mates to come with you and have a go at them.

Sadly there are stupid people around that shout offensive remarks – about the colour of your skin, your race, religion or even just the way you look.

You know that the person saying these things is wrong, but the best thing you can do is keep your dignity (they lost theirs a long time ago) and totally ignore them, no matter how upset you are. If you start having a go at them, you've given them what they wanted – an excuse to come over and take things further.

Note: If you are really worried about comments someone makes, especially if they become threatening, try to memorise the person's appearance, or any other details that could identify them like their car registration number. Then talk to your parents, or another adult and consider contacting the police.

Racial Harassment: This is a serious issue and applies to any verbal, written or physical attacks that have a racial motive. If the attacker is caught they can be prosecuted.

You are walking home with your sister when a car pulls up and a group of lads tell her she's sexy. They start hassling her and you tell them to go away. Then they start threatening you, saying they're going to beat you up and calling you gay. You:
a) both cut down a side street and run off.
b) go over to their car and give them a mouthful.
c) tell your sister to run home, and stand your ground.

Listening to someone abusing you or someone who's with you, is not a pleasant experience. So what should you do? Give them a mouthful back and you might end up in a fight, and get seriously hurt. Ignore them and you might feel like they've won. Run off and you might feel like a coward.

There's no easy answer, except to think long-term about the situation. What's an ideal result? That they go away and you can carry on as before. So what's the best way to achieve this? Walk away. It's the best personal safety device there is. It's not cowardice, it's self-preservation and an assertion of your right to be safe.

If you're faced with an aggressive person, use the following tips:

1) Keep calm – the minute you lose your temper they might go for you.
2) Back away, facing the aggressor, until you get a

safe distance away. This lets you watch what they are doing.

3) Keep a safe distance while talking to them. Do not touch them at all.

4) If things turn violent, get away as fast as you can.

You've been to a party and are walking home through town. You pass a group of lads coming out of a pub. One of them shouts at you, and you try to walk on, ignoring them. But he catches your arm and swings a punch at your head. You:

a) Punch him back really hard before he can hit you.

b) Struggle free from his grip and leg it as fast as you can.

c) Kick him and shout for help.

How many times have you seen a fight? You've probably known someone in one, or been involved in one yourself. Every year, thousands of young people – boys in particular – get seriously hurt, in fights. Unfortunately, there are some people who actually enjoy having fights – waiting to pick on someone for silly things, like pushing, spilling a drink, or getting involved in another argument. If you ever find yourself being attacked, the following advice is worth considering:

1) Think. What you would do? Would you fight back? Would you resist? Or would you try to escape as quickly as possible? It's hard to know, as some people have escaped trouble by fighting back, while others have not. So some people believe it makes it worse if you fight back, and others believe in self-defence. See Chapter 17 for more information on self-defence.

2) Shout. Scream for help, or set off a personal

alarm. This may startle the attacker and make them run off, and it will also attract help.

3) Fight. If you do fight back, you have the legal right to defend yourself 'with reasonable force'. This means you could use anything you have on you, like an umbrella, hairspray, keys, or the heel of your shoe, to fend off the attacker. But this doesn't mean that you should arm yourself with knives or guns on the off-chance that someone may attack you. The law says you can't carry any 'offensive weapons' and if you use them, even in self-defence, there would be trouble.

4) Run away. Above all, get as far away as you can from the situation. You don't have to be a hero – just get out of there and save your own skin.

Real-life story: 'I got jumped on'

I was on my way home one evening, when three boys walked past me and started shouting abuse at me. I tried to ignore it, but they followed me, prodding me and goading me, until I turned round and told them to get lost. With that they jumped on me, and started beating me up. I couldn't fight off three boys – they were bigger than me and they really laid into me. I ended up on the floor covering my head, and they kicked me in the chest so hard that they broke two ribs, and bruised me all over my arms and legs. I also had a black eye. Someone must have called the police, because the next thing I knew they had run off, and the ambulance took me to hospital. The police said I was lucky that I escaped as lightly as I did. But I still don't know why they hit me in the first place.

Jon, 17

What to do if you have been attacked

- **Are you hurt?** If you need help, call out to a passer-by, or try to get to a busy well-lit area, a shop, or a garage. Someone will help you call an ambulance and your parents.
- **Remember.** Try to recall as many details as you can – what the attackers looked like, what they were wearing, or a car make, colour and registration number.
- **Witnesses.** If there were people who saw the attack, it will help if you can try to get their names and numbers, so the police can talk to them later. You might not feel up to it at the time, but if you can get someone to help you do it, it might make a huge difference.
- **Police.** Ask your parents or a friend to help you contact the police. You don't have to go to the police station to report an assault – you can be interviewed from your own home if you want. The police deal with you sympathetically after an attack.

Be aware: Aggression and Assault

In summary, here are the main points to take away from this chapter:

1) Staying silent sometimes means keeping safe.

2) Walking away does not equal cowardice.

3) Racial harassment is against the law.

4) Use anything you have on you for self-defence, but if you carry 'offensive weapons' you might get locked up and the attacker set free.

5) Don't be afraid to involve the police.

Chapter 15

Someone's Following Me

Real-life story: 'I was followed home'

I caught the bus home one winter evening in the dark. This man sat right next to me – I thought he was a bit close, but I didn't say anything – it's always crowded on the bus. I felt a bit odd about him, so I moved seats. He did too – and then he stared at my legs all the way home. I don't know why I didn't say anything to the bus conductor, but in a panic I got off the bus at the wrong stop, and then he followed me. I still think I should have told the conductor and made the bus stop or something, but I just walked off, upset, and the man followed me again. I have never been so scared in my life. I got my mobile out ready, and worked out what I could use to hit him – I'd read you can use the heel of your shoe. I kept turning round and round and he was still there, so in the end I crossed the road and headed to a shopping precinct and I went into a shop and told the owner. He was really nice to me, but the man had gone.

Lynne, 16

If you've ever been followed, you'll know it's a seriously scary experience. Reading about it now, it all seems so straightforward, doesn't it? Lynne should have told the conductor, then stayed with someone else until she was safe. But it's never that straightforward. Like Lynne, you can't be sure, you think you're being silly, or you panic and don't know what to do at all . . .

What to do if you think you're being followed: Your 10-point safety plan

1) Always know where you are going and where you are. If you get lost, go into a shop or garage and ask for help.

2) Trust your instincts. We often tell ourselves we're imagining bad things, but it's better to be safe and wrong any day.

3) If you are followed, speed up your pace and cross the road, looking confident. If the person crosses after you . . .

4) Speed up some more. Don't run, just walk faster.

5) If you have a personal alarm, hold it in your hand. You could also get your mobile out at this point too.

6) Look around for a shop, or a group of people (ideally with women). Explain you are being followed and ask for help.

7) If you can't see anything open or anyone around, walk confidently up to a house with its lights on, as if it's yours. Ring the bell and ask for help. Or dial 999 on your mobile phone.

8) Keep an eye on the person behind you by looking at their reflection in car windows or shop windows. This is better than looking over your shoulder. Try to increase your speed to match theirs.

9) If they start running, it's time to go into emergency mode:

    a) Run as fast as you can.

    b) If you are carrying something heavy, throw it down.

    c) Shout and wave your arms to attract attention.

    d) Set off your personal alarm if you have one.

e) Run towards someone for help – if there are no pedestrians, try to wave down a passing car.

10) Avoid using a public phone box, as they could trap you inside – instead try to use a phone inside a shop or pub, if you don't have a mobile.

What men can do to make women feel safer

It's wrong to think that men never get followed or attacked, as the opposite is more true. All of the above tips apply to boys as much as girls. But have you ever thought you might accidentally scare a girl, by walking behind her in the street, especially at night? Think about the following:

Walk this way: If you're walking right behind a girl who is on her own, you could scare her. Walk on the other side of the road if you can.

Give her space: If you get on a bus or train, try not to sit too close to a woman who is on her own.

Chatting up: If you start talking to a girl in the street, or at a bus stop, she's probably going to be wary. She doesn't know if you are dodgy or safe, so don't be offended if she's rude to you.

Cat calls: If you're with a group of lads and you start cat-calling a girl, whistling or even jostling her, she might be scared and upset by it. You think you're just having a laugh, but she could feel threatened. Try to think about the situation from her point of view.

Walk her home: A really considerate thing you can do for female friends or family is seeing them home safely by giving them a lift or walking them home when you can. Make sure they are safely indoors before you leave them.

Flashers

Flashers are seen as a bit of a joke – just dirty old men in raincoats getting a bit of a thrill by showing off their tackle, right? Maybe, but it's still an unpleasant experience if you come across one. Read this true scenario and think about what you'd do:

I was walking home in the dark with my friend, and we passed a bloke in a gateway. He said 'Excuse me!' and when we turned to look at him, he was masturbating. We told him he was disgusting and ran off, but he followed us, calling us slags. My friend thought it was funny and told me to forget it, but I was upset. I didn't know what to do.

Kerry, 17

What would you do?

a) Laugh it off and forget about it.
b) Call the police and tell them what happened.

This is what Kerry did:

The next day, I told my mum and together we called the police and reported it. They came round and took a description and they were really nice to me and said I was right to call them. They came back with some pictures of suspects – and I spotted him. They did catch him – he'd been doing it to lots of girls.

Note: Most flashers are usually harmless and don't do much more than give their bits and bobs an airing. But flashing is illegal – it's known as 'indecent exposure' and for this reason, anyone caught doing it can be prosecuted.

What to do if you see a flasher

Run off: If someone flashes at you, get away from them as fast as you can. Don't try to confront them.

If you are flashed on public transport, or in an enclosed space, then first move as far away from the person as possible. Try to get other people's attention by shouting. You could say something like, 'You're disgusting!' or 'Pervert'. The flasher will most likely run away after this.

Get help: If you're stuck on a bus or train with a flasher, look for someone to help you, like a family or couple. If it's really dangerous, you could even pull the emergency cord. They can help you talk to the guard, or use the emergency phone on the station platform.

Speak up: The worst thing you could do is keep quiet out of embarrassment or shame – it's not your fault.

Get to a safe place: If the flasher follows you, then go into emergency mode, and get to a safe place immediately.

Report them: Try to remember as much as you can about them – what they looked like or what they were wearing. Then when you get home, your parents can help you contact the police to give a description.

Abduction

Every year you read stories in the papers of teenagers or children that go missing – often last seen walking to or from school, after a night out, or even just playing outside.

Don't talk to strangers. Everyone is taught this when they're little. We all know the classic image of a pervy old man saying, 'Do you want to see my puppies?' and luring you away with a bag of sweets. Then, as you get older you forget about this and think you're perfectly able to look after yourself. But the problem is, 'bad' people don't look like the Child Catcher, or Darth Vader, do they? In fact, sometimes they are so normal, you might actually know them. So, even though you are older, you should still be careful about your own safety.

What to do if someone tries to abduct you

As a rule, always let someone know where you are going and when you will be back. If you think someone is trying to abduct you, remember the tips in Chapter 14 on assault. Then, always:

1) Struggle. Try to get away immediately – do anything you can to get away from them. If you're carrying a bag, chuck it down to help you get away. Actually, leaving something of yours behind might help someone find you.

2) Shout. Scream, try to attract the attention of passers-by, or set off your personal alarm.

3) Pretend someone else is there. You could try shouting any name that comes into your head so the attacker will think there's someone with you that they haven't seen.

4) Fight. Use physical force – see Chapter 17.

5) Dial 999. Use your mobile phone and call for help. Even if you can't talk, you can dial 999 and leave the phone on, without the abductor knowing. Try to make some noise, like talking to the abductor. The police can trace the call and find you this way.

6) Or call someone else. Use your mobile 'Phone Book' or 'Last 10 Calls' to quick-dial anyone else.

7) Text. If you can't make a sound, you can even think about texting someone with things like, 'kdnappd. hlp. white vn, heath rd.'

8) In a car. If you are forced into a car, try to spot the door handle. If you can, unwind the window and shout and attract attention. If you have no luck, when the car stops at traffic lights, unlock the door and leap out as fast as you can. Run for safety, ideally in a busy area, where there are lots of other people.

9) Talk. You could also try to talk to the abductor. Tell them that someone knows where you're going, what you're doing, and when you were meant to get there.

10) Stay calm. This is difficult, but try telling them your name and all about your family and life. The abductor then has time to think, which could help make them think about what they're doing, and have second thoughts about it. It may be the last thing you feel like doing, but it could work.

Be aware: Someone's Following Me

In summary here are the main points to take away from this chapter:

1) Always tell someone where you are going and what time you will be back.

2) Trust your instincts.

3) If you are followed, make your way to a public place and get help.

4) Flashing is a criminal offence, and will be prosecuted.

5) Your mobile phone can be a good emergency tool.

Chapter 16

Rape and Sexual Assault

Q & A: Rape and sexual assault

Q: *What is rape?*
A: It's when someone forces you to have sex against your will – which means in any situation, with anybody or when you don't consent to sex.

Q: *Are most rapes done by strangers?*
A: No, despite the image of someone lurking in the bushes, research shows that in most cases the person being raped knows the attacker.

Q: *Do most rapes happen at night?*
A: No, they don't. That's just a false image of rape that most of us have. In general, most rapes by a stranger happen during the daytime, and rapes by an acquaintance usually happen at night. Plus, about half of all rapes take place in the victim or attacker's home.

Q: *What is date rape?*
A: A few years ago date rape was officially recognised and made illegal. Loads of people debated whether you could actually be raped when you're going out or on a date with someone, and the answer was yes – if you don't consent to sex, no matter what else you may have been doing, it's rape. So date rape is forced sex between partners, dates, friends, friends of friends or acquaintances,

when there's no consent. For more information on date rape, see pages 144–145.

Q: *Does that mean you could also be raped when you're married?*
A: Yes, it does. Husbands can rape their wives – if they force themselves on her when she doesn't consent, then that is rape.

Q: *What about men? Can they be raped too?*
A: Yes, they can. Rape and sexual assault can apply to either sex – a woman can rape a man, and a man can rape another man. Although statistically more rapes are carried out on women, it's important to understand that many victims are men.

Q: *What's the difference between rape and sexual assault?*
A: Not a lot. But the law makes a difference – it classifies rape as when a penis enters the vagina or anus, and sexual assault as sexual contact against a woman or man's will, such as touching, fondling or oral sex.

Q: *What about sexual abuse?*
A: Yes, this counts as rape too. (See pages 66–70 for more information on abuse.) Most men and women who have been sexually abused know their abuser – be it a parent, friend or relative. It's important to remember that no matter how well you know someone or how much you struggle, sexual abuse is always wrong. People who have been abused often feel very confused, as they felt love and trust for their abuser, which causes their emotions to get mixed up.

Myths about rape

Have you ever heard someone telling a joke about rape? The answer's probably yes. Sadly, it's often made into a bit of a joke by people, and not taken seriously. Here are some common myths about rape:

Myth 1: Women say no when they mean yes.

Fact: You might see TV programmes or films where the woman's saying 'No', but the man snogs her some more and she gives in. This is not true – it's important to realise that when someone says no, male or female, they mean it.

Myth 2: Only young, pretty women get raped.

Fact: Women of all ages, race and class are raped. And men get raped too. It has nothing to do with what someone looks like.

Myth 3: If a woman is wearing skimpy clothes, she's asking for it.

Fact: Of course she isn't. No one ever asks to be attacked or violated, whatever they look like or wear.

Myth 4: It's not rape if the person doesn't fight back.

Fact: Wrong again. If someone threatens or intimidates you to have sex through fear, then that is rape. Many people don't fight back for fear of getting hurt even more. Sometimes the victim can be paralysed by fear, but no matter what they do or don't do, the blame lies with the rapist.

Myth 5: If someone's drunk, or stoned, it's not rape.

Fact: If the victim is out of it, then she or he can't give consent to sex, which makes it rape. And it makes no difference how well they know the rapist either. For more information on drug rape, see pages 146–148.

Myth 6: If a boy spends a lot of money on a girl, she owes him sex.

Fact: Even if he gave her a million pounds, she owes him nothing. Why should she? He can't buy her body – that's prostitution. If a boy spends money on a girl, that's his choice. Whether she has sex with him or not, that's her choice.

Myth 7: Rapists just want to have sex.

Fact: It's nothing to do with sex really – rape is all about power, control and anger. Many rapists have partners, or are married already. They just want to dominate and humiliate their victim.

Myth 8: Girls make up stories about being raped to get back at a man.

Fact: This myth is used a lot to show that a girl is lying and that she's making it all up just to get at the bloke. But statistics show that this isn't true at all – only 2% of claims are false, the same as for any crime.

Myth 9: Rapists are not normal.

Fact: Rapists are not all weirdo loners who look like monsters. Many are married, have families, and seem perfectly normal. That's also why when someone is raped by someone they know, they think no one will believe them.

Myth 10: Rape doesn't happen very often.

Fact: Unfortunately, this is not true. According to the Rape Crisis Federation, almost one in four women in the UK have suffered rape or attempted rape – but 91% of women tell no one.

Real-life story: 'I was raped at a swimming pool'

It was summer, and I had been going to my local swimming pool all the holidays. There was this boy there that I really fancied, and over the weeks we'd been talking a lot. One day he followed me into the changing rooms and he started kissing me. I was really pleased – I couldn't believe he'd finally got the message. We got quite passionate, and he shut the door of the cubicle. I was enjoying it, but when he pulled down my bikini top, I pulled away and said I wanted to slow down. He said, 'Come on, you're enjoying it' then pushed me back against the wall and put his hand inside my bikini bottoms. I said no, and told him to stop but before I knew it he was having sex with me. I didn't know what to do – I struggled a bit, and started crying, but he was so heavy, he crushed me against the wall, and carried on until he finished. Then he walked off, laughing. I told my friend and she said she didn't think that counted as rape, as I had been kissing him, so I didn't tell anyone else. I felt really guilty, and cheap, and like it was my fault.

Steph, 16

Note: Steph's friend gave her some bad advice – what happened to her was rape. It didn't matter that she'd been kissing him, or that she fancied him. She didn't want to have sex, she didn't give her consent, so this was rape.

How to avoid being a victim

Trust your instincts: If a situation feels weird – like if the person you are with suddenly gets aggressive or controlling – then go with your feelings on this, and get yourself away from that situation as fast as you can.

Be assertive: Look confident. Many victims are picked because they look vulnerable, so try to look like you know what you're doing and where you're going, even if you don't. It might sound silly, but this includes walking with your back straight, and keeping your hands out of your pockets. See Chapter 17 for more confidence tips.

Avoid dodgy situations: Don't put yourself at risk by walking home late at night on your own, or accepting lifts from strangers.

Think what you would do: Although you might think it's silly or paranoid, pre-planning what you would do if you were ever attacked could help you.

Don't drink too much: If you're really drunk or high, you become an easier target. No one's saying not to have a good time, but try to stay in control of your senses, so you always know what's happening to you. Also, watch out for drinks being spiked, especially at clubs and bars (see pages 146–148).

Stay together: If you're out in a group, stick together and have a meeting point or back-up plan in case you split up.

Know how you're getting home: Always think about how you are getting home. The last thing you want is to be wandering around alone, with no cash or not knowing how you're getting home.

What to do if you are raped or sexually assaulted

If the unthinkable happens, and you are attacked, then having these tips at the back of your mind could help. It's wise to spend a few minutes thinking about what you would do in that situation – as it could give you some crucial seconds in a crisis.

Before:

1) **Try to escape.** If you think you're about to be raped, try to get away as fast as you can. This is where your instincts come into play again – if you feel worried about a situation, then listen to your fears and try to get away. It doesn't matter if your instincts were wrong, afterwards. It is worth listening to your instincts.

2) **Shout.** Although you might not feel like shouting, letting out a big scream could alert someone to come to your help. One rape victim's tip is to shout and scream as loud as you can. She advises shouting 'Fire!' instead of 'Help!' as people are more likely to get involved.

3) **Say no.** Try to say no as clearly and as often as you can. This is especially important if you know the attacker. Shake your head, push them away, scream and scream 'No!', anything you can think of to make them stop.

4) **Fight?** This is a hard question, because it can depend on the situation. Some victims have fought back and escaped, some have saved themselves by

not fighting. There is no right or wrong answer. If they have a weapon, or you think you'll be hurt more by fighting, then it might be safer not to fight at all. Trust your instincts at the time. People who are attacked react in different ways, and all of them are valid reactions. Not fighting back doesn't mean you want to have sex, so never feel guilty about whatever action you do or do not take. If you have a personal alarm, set it off, or you could use self-defence tactics (see Chapter 17).

5) Talk. Sometimes talking can be the answer to stopping an attack. Some victims say that they just babbled on about anything they could think of, to try to reason with the attacker and make them stop. They told them all about their families, or told them that doing this was wrong (especially if they knew them), they kept saying no, they asked the attacker how they would feel if this happened to their mum, daughter or sister. Other people told the attacker they were having their period, had AIDS or another STI, were pregnant or anything they could think of. Try to say anything to put off the attacker.

After:

1) Get help. The first thing to do, is get to safety. If you have been attacked outside, try to get to a safe place – look out for somewhere like a shop or garage that's open, or if you can't see anyone, try attracting the attention of a passer-by, flagging down a car, or even knocking on someone's door. If you have a mobile phone, you could call your family or friends to help.

2) Are you hurt? If you need medical help, someone

can call you an ambulance, and medical staff will contact your family for you.

3) Call a rape crisis centre. The Rape Crisis Federation is a nationwide organisation for anyone who has been raped or sexually assaulted. They can offer advice over the phone, face-to-face counselling, and can also explain the medical and police procedures. They can also send someone to a hospital or police station with you.

4) Go for tests. If you have been raped, then you might need tests for STIs or a pregnancy test. For this it's best if you have someone to support you – family, friends or a counsellor to make it easier for you.

5) Police. It's your decision whether to go to the police or not. Try to weigh up the pros and cons, perhaps with family or friends. There are arguments for and against reporting it to the police – it can be a long process, and you might feel like you've been through enough already. But if no one reported it, then no one would ever get caught. There are special units set up for rape victims with specially trained police officers, who can arrange for a doctor to see you. Ideally, if you want to report the rape, it is better not to wash until you have had an examination, so the police can collect DNA to help catch the attacker. This isn't easy, because when people are raped, often the first thing they want to do is scrub away the attack. You don't have to go into the police station – officers can come to your home and interview you there. They will be sympathetic and kind, and listen to what you say.

Then, it's up to you if you want to press charges and take the case to court. Whatever you decide, it is the right choice for you. Don't feel pressured into doing one thing or the other.

6) Whatever you need. Remember to look after your emotions. Everyone reacts differently to trauma, and there's no right or wrong way to act. Go home, and try to rest and recover with all the love and support of your family and friends. Don't think you have to keep it secret – it will help to talk about it. Let all your feelings out – get mad, cry, shout, whatever you want to do. It's also good to talk to a counsellor, or a support group like the Rape Crisis Federation or Victim Support. See Resources for more details.

How to help someone who has been raped

If you know someone who's been raped, the most important things you could do are:

1) Understand. Be accepting of how they react – whether she or he is blocking it all out, crying a lot, getting angry, feeling like they can't trust anyone. All are normal reactions. Just be there for the person.

2) Listen. They may want to talk about what happened over and over, and you might not want to hear the upsetting details, but the best thing you can do is listen, and let them get it all out – however long it takes. Other people might not want to talk about it at all, and if this happens, it's best not to keep probing.

3) Don't advise. You might think you know what's best for them, but they have to decide for themselves what to do. Help them weigh up their options, instead of forcing them into something, such as going to the police.

4) Don't sulk. If he or she starts ignoring you, and you feel shut out, the worst thing you could do is turn on them and say you need their support. Your feelings are important, but at the moment they can't help you. Instead, you could chat to someone else close to you for advice, or contact a support group yourself.

5) Help practically. You could go with him or her to a clinic, for STI or pregnancy tests, or to the police. You can help organise appointments or go with them, or talk to them about their emotions afterwards.

Date rape dilemma

This is a true story: Sally was at a party, where she was having a really good time. She was drinking and smoking a joint, and chatting to Ben, who she had fancied for a long time. She started to feel out of it, so went upstairs, where she passed out on a bed. She woke up to find Ben on top of her, having sex. He finished, rolled off and left her.

What would you do?

1) Scream and shout, call him a bastard, and run downstairs telling everyone what happened.

2) Corner him and demand to know what he thought he was doing.

3) Go home, ring the police and report him.

4) Cry, tell your friend and try to put it behind you – there's no point telling anyone else, as they wouldn't believe you.

None of these options seem very appealing do they? You

can see the problems with date rape – you say you were raped – hey, you weren't even conscious – but they say you wanted to have sex. There were no witnesses. So how do you prove it really happened? But you know the truth, and you have to live with this for ever.

Date rape facts

- Date rape is forced sex between partners, dates, friends, friends of friends or acquaintances, when there is no consent.
- Date rapists may hurt you physically and emotionally. For example, they might threaten to hit you or hurt you, call you names, say they are going to bad-mouth you all round town, or say bad things about your family.
- If a person is on a date or at a party and has so much to drink that they can't consent to sex, then assaulting them is rape.

Date rape: Do's and Don'ts

Do avoid parties where people are taking a lot of drugs or drink. Studies of date rape show many rapists and victims had been taking drugs or drinking before the attack.
Don't lose control. If you are drinking or using drugs, then try to stay in control as much as possible.
Do avoid people who make you uncomfortable.
Don't leave your mates. If you're at a party, arrange to go with a friend, look out for them all evening and go home with them at the end of the night.
Do say no. If you are not comfortable in any situation say 'NO'. If someone tries to force sex with you, tell them no, and keep saying no. If you feel threatened you could start

screaming and shouting, and using any of the survival tips you have read about.

Don't go off alone with someone you've only just met. Try to stick to the busiest part of the bar, party, or club, and keep close to your friends.

Drug rape

Real-life story: 'My mate's drink was spiked'

Me and my friend were at this club one night, and we were drinking bottles of beer. We had a dance, and then went back for a drink. I felt fine, but my friend started acting really drunk all of a sudden. I thought she was being stupid, and she staggered off to the loo, and then passed out on the floor. Luckily I followed her in and found her and took her home. We called the doctor as she was unconscious, and we'd only had one beer. He told us her drink was spiked with a rape drug and she was really lucky that I was with her.

Vicky, 17

What is drug rape?

Another type of rape in the headlines lately is drug rape. As Vicky discovered, this is when someone spikes your drink with a 'date rape drug'. The way these drugs work is that people slip them into your drinks without you knowing, making you disorientated and appear drunk. Then, often the attacker appears to 'help you' when you start staggering about, but actually takes you off and rapes you. Most times the victim doesn't even know what's happened until they wake up hours later when they notice someone has had sex with them. Sometimes they wake up in someone's bed, who claims they were really drunk, but yes, they were up for it last night. They can't even remember what happened.

This is one of the fastest-growing crimes in the UK – against men and women. These drugs, like Rohypnol, known as 'roofies', are tasteless and odourless, and are quickly processed by the body, often leaving no trace of what has happened.

How to avoid drug rape

The Roofie Foundation provides this advice against drug rape:

- Never leave a drink unattended.
- If someone offers you a drink, try to see it opened and poured.
- If you are in a group, ask the designated driver, or anyone else not drinking, to keep an eye on everyone's drinks.
- Although Rohypnol now has blue dye in it by law that shows up if it is put in your drink, it doesn't show up for 20 minutes, plus you won't be able to see it in dark or bottled drinks.
- If you feel odd, dizzy or wasted and you know you are not drunk, tell a friend and go to safe place.
- Ask someone to stay with you until the effects of the drug have worn off.
- If you are alone, tell a bar or club employee straight away and ask them to fetch your parents or friends to help. Do not rely on a stranger – no matter how helpful they appear. They could have drugged you.

Be aware: Rape and Sexual Assault

In summary, here are the main points to take away from this chapter:

1) Both men and women can be raped and sexually assaulted.

2) 60% of rape victims know their attacker.

3) Date rape is as bad as anonymous rape. No always means no.

4) If you are raped, there is no right or wrong way to react or feel.

5) Be vigilant when drinking in bars, clubs or at parties. Drug rape is one of the fastest-growing crimes in Britain.

Chapter 17

Confidence

This book has covered many of the aspects of modern day life that you need to know about to be streetwise. If you read the whole book from start to finish in one go (unlikely, but maybe you're a speed reader!), you may well be thinking, 'Oh, great, I'll just barricade myself inside my house and never go out again as you've freaked me out so much. Thanks.' Hopefully you don't feel like this, because as we said at the start of the book – it is very likely that none of these things will ever happen to you. It's simply about being aware.

Being aware of the realities of life with all its risks will make you prepared and ultimately more confident conducting yourself in different situations. That's what this chapter is about – the things you can do to boost your confidence and remain alert. Remember, be aware not beware.

The secret power of confidence

What's your number-one self-defence tool? No, not a machete, or bazooka, but confidence. It's been proven that attackers are less likely to go for people who look confident. It's all about looking confident – looking like you know where you are going, are sure of yourself and can look after yourself.

But this is not to say that feeling afraid is wrong. The whole reason we have a fear mechanism is to warn our bodies of danger and to help us get out of situations as soon as possible. Our bodies use fear to escape – when you start feeling worried, your brain starts adrenaline pumping through your body, which acts like a power-boost, letting you run away faster.

So what's better – to ignore your fear and stay there, running the risk that something may happen to you, or leg it and be sure to be safe? Trust your instincts. If you ever think something is wrong, it's better to go with that thought and clear out as soon as possible.

Body language

You don't have to walk down the road shouting, 'Hi, my name is John, and I'm really confident, you know,' to show people that you're strong. In fact you don't need to say anything at all – it's all in your body language. (And actually, sometimes people can say one thing, but their body language says another.)

Body language tells people a lot – it can tell someone you are nervous (foot tapping, leg jiggling), fibbing (touching your face while talking) or attracted to them ('imaginary grooming' such as rubbing fingers through hair). It can also tell people you feel confident. So here's how to give off body signals that show you are confident, even when you are not:

1) **Walk briskly,** and look like you have a purpose, or know where you are going, even when you don't.
2) **Stand up straight,** with your head held high and shoulders back. Slouching and staring at the pavement tells everyone that you lack confidence.
3) **Keep your hands out of your pockets,** and out of your sleeves, and swing them by your sides. Don't fold your arms.

4) Try to walk properly. Shuffling your feet or dragging them along, or walking with your feet close together or your toes pointing inwards can make you look less confident (and maybe even have less balance). Also, try to wear shoes you can walk and run in easily, like trainers.

5) If you are feeling nervous and agitated, try to tell your body to calm down. Take deep breaths and count to ten, which can relax your muscles and relieve your tension.

6) Look where you're going. Keep your head up and look ahead of you, as opposed to watching the pavement. Not only do you look more confident, but you can see what's coming.

7) Don't fidget. If you are sitting down, or standing still, try to do just that. Things like frantic leg jiggling, fidgeting with rings or jewellery, biting your nails, picking at your lips, or face, or wringing hands makes you look nervous and vulnerable.

8) Make eye contact. No, not a staring match, but it's better to look at people if you need to talk to them, or move past them, as opposed to shuffling past with your head down. Again, this body language would make you look nervous and unconfident.

Q & A: Self-defence

Some people may think that the safest thing to do is learn self-defence, so that in any risky situation you can defend yourself. It can help you feel more confident and safe and could help you defend yourself in a worst-case scenario. If you are considering taking self-defence classes, here are a few of your questions answered:

Q: *What is self-defence?*
A: It's not just fighting. It teaches you awareness and assertiveness skills. It helps you know what to say in confrontations and gives you safety strategies. It also teaches you techniques to prevent, avoid, escape and resist physical assaults. A good self-defence course provides psychological awareness training as well as physical training.

Q: *Does self-defence work?*
A: It increases your options and prepares you to avoid, slow-down or escape a physical attack, and boosts your confidence. And don't forget that many attacks are from people you know, not always strangers, and these techniques can help with these.

Q: *Does self-defence guarantee you will be safe?*
A: No! There are no guarantees that you will be 100% safe and a good self-defence course will tell you this. If you are attacked, whether or not you fight back depends on the situation. You may feel confident to perform a few moves that you have been taught, or you may not. You see, it all depends on the circumstances at the time. There may be one attacker, or there could be many. They may have weapons, or they may not. There is no right or wrong answer in self-defence. Sometimes the best defence is to walk or run away.

Where can I find out about courses in my area?
Your local police station should have details about self-defence classes. Also try your local community centre, or look in the Yellow Pages.

Self-defence tips

If you do fight back here are a few moves that might help:

- Aim for a tender area – kick/punch knee-caps, shins, testicles.
- Pull back the attacker's little finger.
- Kick or punch the attacker's Adam's apple.
- Poke your finger in the attacker's eye.
- Push your palm up under the attacker's nose, really hard.
- Scratch, bite.
- As soon as you try something, don't wait to see if it hurt, just wriggle free and run off.

Safety equipment

Personal alarms: You might think about buying a personal alarm to keep in your bag at all times. They are not very expensive and you can buy them from most DIY stores. The Suzy Lamplugh Trust has a good model that you can buy online or through mail order. See Resources for contact numbers.

Personal alarms are simple to use – when you feel in danger you press a button to activate it, and it lets out an ear-piercing, high-pitched shriek, that should scare off the attacker or startle them enough for you to get away or get help.

Weapons: No matter how tempted you may be to arm yourself with weaponry to ward off any would-be attackers, remember that carrying anything that can be described as an 'offensive weapon' is illegal. The law does not allow you to march around the street with a carving knife, machete or hammer, for example. This is for the safety of all of us, but also think about how it could go wrong – if you drew a knife at a would-be attacker, they could possibly turn it round and use it on you, and then claim self-defence. It's an area best avoided.

Using personal belongings: If the worst came to the worst and you were attacked, the law allows you to defend yourself, using reasonable force with any item you have to hand (offensive weapons excluded). So you could grab anything that's on you – an umbrella, keys, hairspray, or your shoe to defend yourself against the attacker.

Mobile phones: And don't forget your phone. You can always dial 999 even with the keypad locked, so you can get help as quickly as possible.

Be aware: Confidence Tips

In summary, here are the main points to take away from this chapter:

1) Confidence is your best self-defence.
2) You can train your body to look confident, even when you're not.
3) Self-defence is not just about fighting.
4) It's illegal to carry 'offensive weapons', so using a knife in self-defence could land you in trouble, not the attacker.

Resources

Where to go for more help

CONTRACEPTION AND STIs

Brook
Free confidential sex advice and contraception for young people: 0800 0185 023. www.brook.org.uk

The Family Planning Association
For confidential sex advice and contraception
FPA England 0845 310 1334
FPA Scotland 0141 576 5088
FPA Wales 029 20 644034
FPA Northern Ireland 028 90 325488
www.fpa.org.uk

STI (Sexually Transmitted Infections) or GUM (Genito-Urinary Medicine) clinics
For your nearest clinics, check your phone book. They are usually attached to a hospital.

National AIDS helpline
Confidential advice on HIV and AIDS. Calls are free and won't show up on your phone bill: 0800 567 123.

Avert (AIDS Education & Research Trust)
Provides free information service on HIV, AIDS and related matters: 01403 210202. www.avert.org

DRUGS

The National Drugs Helpline
Info and advice for people who misuse drugs, or for family and friends: 0800 77 66 00. www.ndh.org.uk

Release
For any advice on drugs: 020 7729 9904. www.release.org.uk

Narcotics Anonymous
A community-based organisation for recovering addicts: 020 7730 0009. www.ukna.org

Re-Solv (Society for the Prevention of Solvent and Volatile Substance Abuse)
Info and support for anyone concerned with substance abuse: 0808 800 2345. www.re-solv.org

The Roofie Foundation
For advice and help concerning date rape drugs: 0800 783 2980. www.roofie.org.uk

ALCOHOL

Alcoholics Anonymous
A support-group for people who wish to stop drinking – including teenagers. Look in your local phone book, or call: 01904 644026. www.alcoholics-anonymous.org.uk

Alateen
Alcoholics anonymous family groups – for families and friends of problem drinkers: 020 7403 0888. www.hexnet.co.uk/alonon

Drinkline
For advice on sensible drinking: 0800 917 8282. www.wrecked.co.uk

VIOLENT CRIME

Rape Crisis Federation
For advice and support on rape and sexual abuse/assault: 0115 934 8474. www.rapecrisis.co.uk

Rape and Sexual Abuse Support Centre (RASASC)
Free confidential advice and support for women and girls who have been raped or abused, no matter how long ago: 020 8683 3300. www.rasasc.org.uk

Lifeline
Help for victims of violence in the home, abuse and incest: 01262 469 085.

Survive
Online help and advice for those who have survived rape and sexual assault, male or female. www.survive.org.uk

Survivors
Help for men who have been sexually assaulted or raped: 020 7357 6677. www.survivorsuk.co.uk

Victim Support
Help for anyone who has suffered from crime:
0845 30 30 900. www.victimsupport.com

BULLYING

Kidscape
For help and advice on bullying: 08451 205204.
www.kidscape.org.uk

Anti-bullying Campaign
For help and advice: 020 7378 1446.

Pupiline
A website for pupils, by pupils, on bullying and other issues:
www.pupiline.co.uk

Bullying Online
An online and email advice centre for anyone concerned about
bullying: www.bullying.co.uk

GENERAL

BT Malicious Phone Call Advice Line
0800 666 700.

Get Connected
Support for young people on any issue, and free connection to
services that can help: 0800 096 0096.

ChildLine
Free 24-hours-a-day helpline for any young person with a
problem: 0800 1111.
www.childline.org.uk

theSite
An online site for young people about all aspects of their lives
– including sex, STIs and drugs.
www.thesite.org.uk

Youth Access
They can refer you to appropriate counselling or service anywhere in the UK, whatever your problem: 020 8772 9900.

The Samaritans
24-hours-a-day help: 08457 90 90 90.
www.samaritans.org.uk

The British Association for Counselling
For help finding a counsellor call: 01788 550899.
www.bac.co.uk

Equal Opportunities Commission
For advice on sexual harassment: 08456 015901.
www.eoc.org.uk

NSPCC Child Protection Helpline
For help and advice on ill-treatment and abuse of children: 0808 800 5000. www.nspcc.org.uk – kids help information – www.there4me.com

Suzy Lamplugh Trust
A national charity for personal safety: 020 8876 0305. www.suzylamplugh.org

ChatDanger
How to chat safely online: www.chatdanger.com

Index